SIERRA SUMMITS

Snow crowns the High Sierra in early summer.

Mount Ritter and Banner Peak tower over the Mammoth Lakes area.

SIERRA SUMMITS

A GUIDE TO FIFTY PEAK EXPERIENCES IN CALIFORNIA'S RANGE OF LIGHT

Matt Johanson

FALCONGUIDES

GUILFORD, CONNECTICUT

FALCONGUIDES®

An imprint of The Rowman & Littlefield Publishing Group, Inc.
4501 Forbes Blvd., Ste. 200
Lanham, MD 20706
www.rowman.com

Falcon and FalconGuides are registered trademarks and Make Adventure Your Story is a trademark of The Rowman & Littlefield Publishing Group, Inc.

Distributed by NATIONAL BOOK NETWORK

Copyright © 2019 Matt Johanson
Photos by Matt Johanson unless otherwise noted
Maps by The Rowman & Littlefield Publishing Group, Inc.

British Library Cataloguing in Publication Information available

Library of Congress Cataloging-in-Publication Data available

ISBN 978-1-4930-3644-8 (paperback)
ISBN 978-1-4930-3645-5 (e-book)

∞™ The paper used in this publication meets the minimum requirements of American National Standard for Information Sciences—Permanence of Paper for Printed Library Materials, ANSI/NISO Z39.48-1992.

Printed in the United States of America

Native Americans discovered and first climbed these mountains. Though their names are unknown, they occupied my thoughts as I followed in their footsteps. This book is for them.

Mobius Arch in
Alabama Hills frames
Lone Pine Peak.

CONTENTS

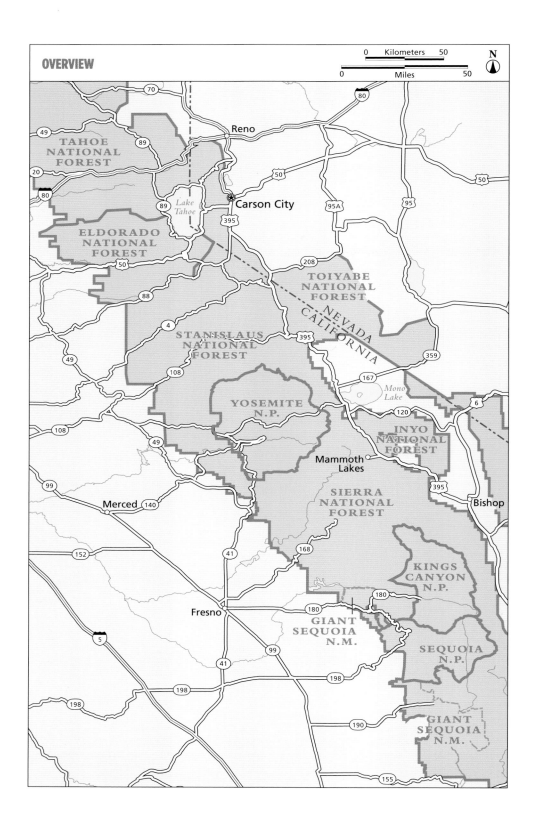

INTRODUCTION TO THE SIERRA NEVADA

Mount Ritter made us fight for every foot. On the upper flanks, a sea of dirt and scree set us back one step for every two we took. But my brother and I could not quit on the mountain we climbed for our dad.

Tom Johanson climbed the same mountain with his Scout troop in 1952, when he was just 14 years old. Two weeks and 137 miles long, that journey took him through Yosemite, Ansel Adams Wilderness, and Sierra National Forest. After he died at age 77, Dan Johanson and I set out to re-create his teenage adventure as a tribute to him. The 13,157-foot summit of Mount Ritter provided the greatest challenge of our outing.

Loose rock, thin air, and route-finding challenges tested our resolve, but with thighs and lungs burning, we reached the rocky summit by early afternoon. We felt weary but joyful, and, most importantly, close to Dad. From the mountaintop he had achieved sixty-three years earlier, we called our mom to include her in the moment, drinking in the grand view of the mountains that our family loves.

The Sierra Nevada range runs 400 miles long and up to 80 miles wide. California's tallest mountains tower above millions of acres of pristine wilderness, encompassing two national monuments, three national parks, and nine national forests. Though Native Americans inhabited this region for millennia, Spanish missionaries applied the name *Sierra Nevada*, meaning "snow-covered mountain range," starting in 1776.

This is where Dad taught us camping, backpacking, and fishing from a young age. Our mom Diane Johanson grew up with special memories from Lake Tahoe and introduced us to that extraordinary place. I grew up in the Bay Area but moved to Tuolumne County for a reporting job at the *Union Democrat* newspaper as a young adult in 1994. Living in the foothills town of Sonora, I discovered Yosemite and rock climbing and got reacquainted with the pleasures of hiking and backpacking.

All of these pursuits took me to the mountains, and starting in my mid-20s, they often led to mountain summits. I reveled in reaching the airy pinnacles of Yosemite's Cathedral Peak, Half Dome, and Clouds Rest with friends and family.

Climbing the 14,505-foot Mount Whitney for the first time in 1997 rates as another special memory. Our group included my cousins Peter and Maggie and my Uncle Ted, Dad's

Author Matt Johanson and his father, Tom Johanson, enjoy a visit to Yosemite.

Tom Johanson and companions summited Mount Ritter in 1952.

brother, who had taught my brothers and me to ski. We pushed ourselves so hard on the John Muir Trail that summiting together felt like an exhilarating achievement.

That adventure woke me to possibilities beyond Yosemite. I began climbing more peaks of the Eastern Sierra (Lone Pine Peak, Mount Conness, and Banner Peak), Lake Tahoe (Mount Tallac, Pyramid Peak, and Sierra Buttes) and Kings Canyon and Sequoia National Parks (Big Baldy and Alta Peak).

Several summits proved challenging, like Mount Lyell and Mount Russell. These provided hard-earned victories, a few character-building setbacks, and plenty of blisters, bruises, and sore muscles. I'm glad I did them, even if I drove home from some swearing "Never again!"

But I also discovered that abundant other mountains offer rewarding experiences without demanding as much blood, sweat, and toil. Lembert Dome, Ebbetts Peak, and Fresno Dome are examples of this inviting variety suitable for beginners and children. Some attract cross-country skiers and snowshoers, like Elephants Back and Martis Peak. Others provide favorable outings for cyclists or hikers with dogs. The Sierra Nevada range, which conservationist John Muir called "the gentle wilderness," really does have something for everyone. For the most part, these adventures are available on public lands for free.

My dad inspired and participated in many other trips, journeying with me on an earlier Mount Ritter effort, to Vogelsang Peak and numerous other destinations, before he died in 2015. The Mount Whitney outing was the last I shared with Uncle Ted, who climbed cheerfully despite a terminal cancer diagnosis, and died the following year. I think they would both be pleased that more bonding moments followed (and continue) involving family and friends in the mountains we love. Mom takes her children and grandchildren on an annual Lake Tahoe vacation. Cousin Peter Johansson hosts a cross-country ski weekend each year at the cabin his parents built. I've delighted in introducing

Dan Johanson and Matt Johanson followed their father's footsteps on Mount Ritter.

Yosemite to my goddaughter Linnae Johansson. Cousin Andy Padlo and I have climbed more mountains together than we can count, and my wife Karen and I enjoy visiting Pinecrest Lake every summer.

Producing *Sierra Summits* has also been a privilege and a joy, leading me to revisit favorite places, discover new areas, climb with old friends, and make new ones. By sharing it, I hope to provide others with the inspiration and the means to enjoy the Range of Light as much as I do.

GEOLOGY

Processes that date as far back as 100 million years created the Sierra Nevada mountains as we now know them. Geologists believe that subduction (the process of one tectonic plate overriding another) and the melting of plates produced magma. Some of this magma rose to the surface and erupted in volcanoes, but most of it cooled miles below the surface, forming compact, crystalline granite. For tens of millions of years the ancestral Sierra Nevada was a high chain of volcanoes, but eventually the tectonic action ceased and the mountains eroded down, exposing the granite beneath them. Faulting and uplift over the past 10 million years raised the mountains to their present elevations.

WEATHER

Summer and early fall provide long days, warm temperatures, and the most favorable conditions for climbing peaks. Mountain passes typically open in late May, and prime climbing season runs from June through October, give or take a month. However, the Sierra Nevada offers no guarantees concerning weather, even in warm seasons. Rain,

Emigrant Wilderness offers nearly limitless adventure opportunities.

hail, and snow can fall on every day of the year. Afternoon thundershowers are common in August, and lightning can be deadly. For this reason, starting early on longer routes improves prospects for successful outings.

Winter and spring bring snow, cold, an early sunset, and far fewer climbers scaling mountains. Yet some of this collection's outings make wonderful winter adventures in the right conditions for those adept in cross-country skiing or snowshoeing. The best time to attempt them is a week or more after heavy snowfall. This gives powder time to settle, reduces avalanche danger, and makes trail breaking easier; driving to and from the mountains will be safer and faster, too.

Average summer temperatures run from 58 degrees at night to 91 degrees during the day. During the winter, temperatures average 30 degrees at night to 54 degrees during the day. The northern part of the range and higher elevations see colder temperatures and more snow. Visitors can obtain weather information from the National Weather Service (weather.gov) and from park and forest websites, entrance stations, and visitor centers.

FLORA AND FAUNA

The Sierra Nevada range contains incredible biological diversity and thousands of species, some found nowhere else on Earth. Learning to identify even a few will enhance appreciation of this ecosystem. Below is an introduction to a few key flora and fauna arranged from most to least agreeable.

Giant sequoias are the largest trees and among the tallest and oldest living things in the world. They grow to more than 300 feet tall and beyond 3,000 years in age, but only do so on the western side of the Sierra Nevada range, and mostly in the south. The sixty-five named groves are concentrated between 4,600 and 7,000 feet of elevation. Record-breaking trees like General Sherman in Sequoia National Park draw legions of admirers, but one can find equally worthy and less-visited trees by hiking short distances.

Sierra bighorn sheep, bald eagles, and California condors all tie for second on this list. Each could have placed first, but the three species are rare and hard to spot, despite recent gains for all of them.

An endangered species since 2000, Sierra bighorns have rebounded from about 100 surviving animals to roughly 600. Separating the bighorns from domestic sheep, which spread fatal diseases to their cousins, has been critical to their recovery. They are most numerous in the Eastern Sierra near Bishop.

Bald eagles and California condors, both endangered and near extinct due to hunting and DDT, are also recovering. Eagles have increased in number enough to be removed from both the endangered and threatened species lists. They are most common near lakes in the Northern Sierra. Condors are still critically endangered but have rebounded from 22 birds in 1987 to some 450 today. Some roosted in Blue Ridge National Wildlife Refuge in the Southern Sierra in 2017 for the first time in forty years.

Black bears are abundant and especially concentrated in popular areas like Yosemite and Lake Tahoe. While black bears do not attack people like grizzlies sometimes do, they are a concern for campers and drivers. Yosemite and other communities have greatly reduced human–bear conflicts by requiring food and trash storage in bear-proof containers. Drivers remain a problem, though, and automobile–bear collisions are on the rise, recently exceeding 100 reported accidents per year in California. Please protect bears by observing speed limits and by securing food and trash while staying in their habitats.

Mosquitoes pose an annoyance in spring and summer varying in degree from mild to insufferable. Many deal with these pesky blood-suckers using nets and chemicals; long-sleeved shirts and long pants are helpful, too. Others time their visits to avoid the flying insects. Their annual life cycle varies: A dry year means a short and early mosquito season, and conversely, a big snow year means more mosquitoes, which survive later into summer and even fall. Mosquitoes hatch first at low elevations and work their way up the mountains as snow melts. Their numbers are greatest near standing water. Good luck!

Poison oak is thankfully rare in these mountains because the oily plant that imparts an itchy rash does not grow above 5,000 feet. Still, visitors should learn to recognize the shrub that sprouts leaves of three. The leaves are green in spring and summer, red in autumn, and fall off the plant in winter, but the stems are still dangerous! It's a good idea to avoid touching any suspicious plant below 5,000 feet, and if you do touch one, wash your skin and clothes.

Finishing our list of notable species, giardia has infected water sources and sickened visitors. While some may dispute the need for this, officials recommend boiling water or treating it with iodine in order to kill the microscopic parasite. This will prevent symptoms like diarrhea or cramps. Generally, water at low elevations (especially beneath camping areas or livestock) is more likely to be infected than high-altitude snowmelt. Take the means to purify water and err on the side of caution.

Sunset paints a beautiful sky above Lake Tahoe.

RESTRICTIONS AND REGULATIONS

Good news! Most outings in this collection require no permit for day use, with a few noteworthy exceptions like Mount Whitney and Half Dome. Those who wish to camp near a glorious mountain summit need wilderness permits from park or forest offices. These are usually free, although some land agencies charge a small fee for reservations.

Several distinctions between national forests and national parks are worth knowing. In forests, camping on undeveloped land is legal, free, and a great way to go. Dogs are legal and there are no entrance fees. Within national parks, visitors must camp in developed campgrounds or in the backcountry (with a permit). Dogs are legal only on leash and in developed areas. You'd better believe there are entrance fees—one charged per car, per week in Yosemite, Kings Canyon, and Sequoia National Parks, or a blanket fee for an annual pass to all national parks and monuments. These are available at the parks and also at https://store.usgs.gov/pass.

Finally, climbers making winter or spring attempts on several summits described as "winter-worthy" (like Castle Peak, Red Lake Peak, or Elephants Back) will need Sno-Park passes to use the parking areas nearest the trailheads. Day-use (or per-season) fees apply, although they are not sold at the unstaffed parking areas. Local retailers may offer them, but the surest move is to get yours in advance at www.ohv.parks.ca.gov/snoparks.

USING THIS GUIDE

Mountain hikes within each of this book's five geographic sections start with the easiest outings and build up to the most difficult ones.

As a guide to mountain hikes that do not require climbing gear, this book uses little specialized vocabulary that needs explanation. But each outing's terrain does get classified according to the following standard definitions:

- Class 1: Easy walking
- Class 2: Simple scrambling on hilly or rough territory
- Class 3: Scrambling on steep ground using handholds and footholds
- Class 4: Simple climbing on steeper and harder terrain with fall potential
- Class 5: Climbing requiring gear, ropes, and belays for protection

Each trip's classification represents the most difficult part of the recommended hike. The vast majority of all fifty featured trips is Class 1 ground. A few mountains have Class 2 or Class 3 terrain near their summits (usually a small amount). None of the suggested outings require Class 4 or Class 5 climbing.

- Hikes described as "family-friendly" are suitable for children at least 10 years old.
- Areas described as "dog-friendly" may still have leash rules.
- Mountains described as "could be campy" require wilderness permits for overnight travel.
- Areas described as "free" have no entrance, permit, or parking fees.

Wildfire prevention is everyone's responsibility. Campfires contribute to wildfires and are restricted in certain park, forest, and wilderness areas. Please learn and abide by local rules and practice fire safety.

Finally, while the author has attempted to make this guide as accurate as possible, users of this book are solely responsible for trip planning, assessing conditions, and their own safety. The outings and activities described in this book involve risk.

Map Legend

Municipal

- ⌗⟨80⟩⌗   Interstate Highway
- ⌗⟨395⟩⌗   US Highway
- ⌗⟨180⟩⌗   State Road
- ⌗⟨506⟩⌗   County/Forest Road
- = = = =   Unpaved Road
- ---·---   State Boundary

Trails

- -------   Featured Trail
- ------   Trail
- ··········   Off-trail Route

Water Features

-   Lake/Reservoir
-   River/Creek
-   Intermittent Stream
-   Waterfall

Symbols

- ⌣   Bridge
- ▲   Campground
- ⊛   Capital
- ▬   Lodging
- ⌇   Pass
- ▲   Peak/Elevation
- 🛆   Picnic Area
- ▪   Point of Interest/Structure
- 🏂   Ski Area
- ♜   Tower
- ○   Town
- ①   Trailhead
- ◪   Viewpoint/Overlook
- ❓   Visitor/Information Center

Land Management

-   National Forest/Park
-   WIlderness Area

PEAK FINDER

DOG FRIENDLY

★ Note: Leash rules may apply.

1. Lovers Leap
4. Mount Rose
5. Castle Peak
7. Freel Peak
8. Ralston Peak
11. Ebbetts Peak
12. Folger Peak

13. Elephants Back
14. Pinecrest Peak
15. Thunder Mountain
16. Mount Reba
17. Red Lake Peak
18. Sonora Peak

20. Round Top
22. Fresno Dome
35. Mitchell Peak
41. Reversed Peak
43. Trail Peak

FAMILY FRIENDLY

★ Suitable for children 10 years old and older

1. Lovers Leap
2. Martis Peak
3. Eureka Peak
6. Sierra Buttes
11. Ebbetts Peak
12. Folger Peak

21. Sentinel Dome
22. Fresno Dome
23. Lembert Dome
24. Gaylor Park
31. Buck Rock
32. Buena Vista Peak

33. Moro Rock
34. Big Baldy
36. The Watchtower
41. Reversed Peak

SUPER SCENIC

5. Castle Peak
6. Sierra Buttes
9. Mount Tallac
10. Pyramid Peak
13. Elephants Back
19. Dardanelles West
21. Sentinel Dome
23. Lembert Dome

25. North Dome
26. Mount Hoffmann
27. Clouds Rest
28. El Capitan
29. Eagle Peak
33. Moro Rock
35. Mitchell Peak

36. The Watchtower
37. Panther Peak
38. Lookout Peak
39. Alta Peak
44. Mount Starr
45. Mount Dana
46. Mount Conness

1. Lovers Leap
3. Eureka Peak
4. Mount Rose
6. Sierra Buttes
7. Freel Peak
8. Ralston Peak
9. Mount Tallac
11. Ebbetts Peak

12. Folger Peak
14. Pinecrest Peak
15. Thunder Mountain
18. Sonora Peak
19. Dardanelles West
22. Fresno Dome
41. Reversed Peak

42. Mammoth Mountain
43. Trail Peak
44. Mount Starr
47. Hurd Peak
49. Matterhorn Peak

25. North Dome
30. Half Dome
32. Buena Vista Peak

33. Moro Rock
34. Big Baldy

42. Mammoth Mountain

10. Pyramid Peak
19. Dardanelles West
24. Gaylor Peak
37. Panther Peak

38. Lookout Peak
40. Sawtooth Peak
45. Mount Dana
46. Mount Conness

47. Hurd Peak
48. Lone Pine Peak

4. Mount Rose (10,776 feet)
7. Freel Peak (10,881 feet)
17. Red Lake Peak (10,063 feet)
18. Sonora Peak (11,459 feet)
20. Round Top (10,381 feet)
24. Gaylor Peak (11,004 feet)

26. Mount Hoffmann (10,850 feet)
35. Mitchell Peak (10,365 feet)
39. Alta Peak (11,204 feet)
40. Sawtooth Peak (12,343 feet)
42. Mammoth Mountain (11,053 feet)
43. Trail Peak (11,617 feet)

44. Mount Starr (12,835 feet)
45. Mount Dana (13,057 feet)
46. Mount Conness (12,590 feet)
47. Hurd Peak (12,237 feet)
48. Lone Pine Peak (12,949 feet)
49. Matterhorn Peak (12,280 feet)
50. Mount Whitney (14,505 feet)

BRAGGING RIGHTS

9. Mount Tallac
10. Pyramid Peak
26. Mount Hoffmann
27. Clouds Rest

28. El Capitan
29. Eagle Peak
30. Half Dome
38. Lookout Peak
39. Alta Peak

40. Sawtooth Peak
48. Lone Pine Peak
49. Matterhorn Peak
50. Mount Whitney

BIKEABLE

2. Martis Peak
14. Pinecrest Peak

15. Thunder Mountain

16. Mount Reba
31. Buck Rock

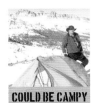

COULD BE CAMPY

★ Wilderness permits required.

20. Round Top
25. North Dome
27. Clouds Rest

28. El Capitan
29. Eagle Peak
30. Half Dome

36. The Watchtower
50. Mount Whitney

WINTER WORTHY

★ Cross-country skis or snowshoes

2. Martis Peak
3. Eureka Peak
5. Castle Peak
8. Ralston Peak
13. Elephants Back

16. Mount Reba
17. Red Lake Peak
21. Sentinel Dome
23. Lembert Dome
31. Buck Rock

32. Buena Vista Peak
34. Big Baldy
37. Panther Peak

Mount Tallac's summit affords a grand view of Lake Tahoe.

LAKE TAHOE

Mark Twain minced no words when describing his first sighting of Lake Tahoe, which he and a companion hiked for at least 20 miles, climbing over a mountain "three or four thousand miles high, apparently," to reach.

"At last the Lake burst upon us, a noble sheet of blue water lifted 6,300 feet above the level of the sea, and walled in by a rim of snow-clad mountain peaks that towered aloft full 3,000 feet higher still!" the author wrote after his 1861 visit. "I thought it must surely be the fairest picture the whole earth affords . . . The air up there in the clouds is very pure and fine, bracing and delicious. And why shouldn't it be? It is the same the angels breathe."

GEOLOGY

Faulting led to the formation of the Lake Tahoe Basin. During a period of tremendous uplifting, the Sierra Nevada range rose to its west. A second fault to the east became the Carson Range. Lava from the now-dormant volcano Mount Pluto formed a natural dam to the north. Rain and snowfall that filled the basin made a lake that was actually hundreds of feet deeper than the present lake, until water eroded the lava dam and formed the Truckee River, Tahoe's only outlet. Then glaciers formed and carved canyons into the western side of the basin, leaving behind stark mountains and such scenic landmarks as Fallen Leaf Lake and Emerald Bay.

Lake Tahoe's elevation of 6,225 feet and its accordingly cold water discourage algae and moss, explaining its dreamy blue color. With 72 miles of shoreline and depths up to 1,645 feet, Tahoe is the second-deepest lake in the United States, and the largest high-elevation lake in North America.

HISTORY

Native peoples have inhabited the lake basin for at least 10,000 years, according to archaeological evidence. Among them are the Washoe, whose name means "the people from here," who believe the coyote Gewe brought them there at the beginning of time. Lt. John Fremont became the first known European American to spot the lake in 1854. California initially recognized it as Lake Bigler after the state's third governor. But the Washoe called it *Da ow a ga,* which European Americans altered to "Tahoe," and that's the name that prevailed.

When miners discovered the Comstock Lode of silver near Virginia City in 1858, a boom in population and construction changed the area forever. Newcomers displaced most Washoe from their ancestral homes by 1862. Loggers cut most trees in the lake basin to support mining and construction between 1860 and 1890. Many Chinese immigrants made a living this way, while Basque (European immigrants from France and Spain) found work as shepherds.

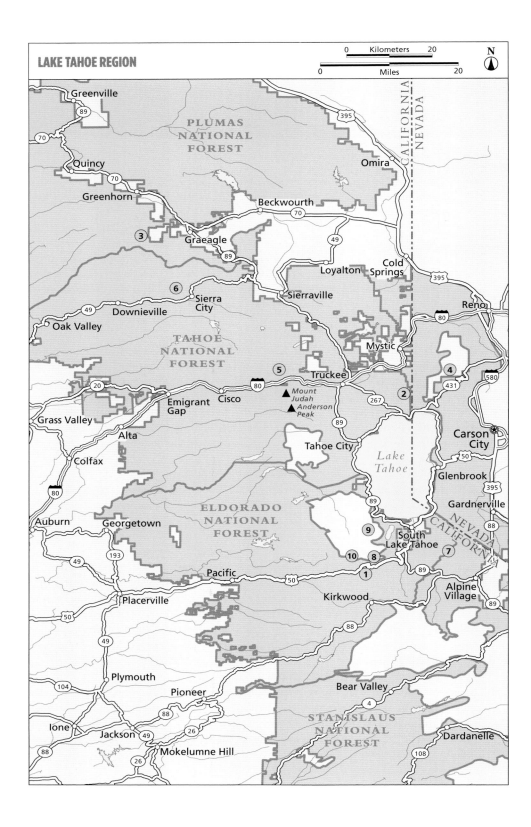

Settlers made their way over Donner Pass north of the lake starting in 1844. The Donner Party attempted to cross in November of 1846, only to be trapped by heavy snowfall near modern-day Truckee. Central Pacific Railroad completed a transcontinental route through here in 1868. I-80 eventually followed, providing the most traveled and accessible route over the mountains, ironically passing right by the Donner Party's ill-fated camp, where nearly half its number starved and froze.

Population growth and development continued around Lake Tahoe in the twentieth century. The first car arrived in 1905. Lodges, restaurants, and taverns soon followed as the area became a favorite tourist destination. After Nevada legalized gambling in 1931, casinos quickly spread on the Silver State side of the lake. The 1960 Winter Olympics at nearby Squaw Valley led to improved highway access. The population grew by five times in the following twenty years.

The Lake Tahoe area has produced its share of significant people who have made their marks in a variety of fields. Among the Washoe, Henry Rupert was known as a shaman and healer, and Dat So La Lee was a renowned basket weaver. About fifteen area residents served in the 10th Mountain Division in World War II. One of these was Jim Winthers, who formed Disabled Sports USA Far West, which helps disabled veterans pursue athletic pursuits like skiing, and has sprouted 120 chapters nationwide. Cyclist Greg LeMond won the Tour de France three times. Skier Tamara McKinney competed in three Winter Olympics, won nine national titles, and became the first American woman to win a World Cup skiing title in 1983. Skier Julia Mancuso won three medals in three Winter Olympics, including a gold in 2006. Snowboarder Jamie Anderson won three medals, including two golds in the 2014 and 2018 Winter Olympics. Major League Baseball star Matt Williams made five All-Star teams and played in three World Series, winning his last in 2001.

Guitarist Trey Stone reached the Rhythm and Blues Music Hall of Fame. Dick Penniman taught about avalanche safety for more than thirty years, helped prevent countless serious accidents, and reached the California Outdoors Hall of Fame. So did Justin Lichter, who hiked and skied the entire Pacific Crest Trail in winter, a first. Cheryl and Tom Milham founded Lake Tahoe Wildlife Care to rehabilitate injured and orphaned animals. Wanda Batchelor became the first woman elected as Washoe tribal leader. Finally, Bill Evers and Jim McClatchy started a movement that succeeded in preserving the lake when the nation's leadership could not.

Members of Congress tried and failed to make the lake basin a national park. Alarmed at environmental threats, Evers and McClatchy founded the League to Save Lake Tahoe, which fought to "Keep Tahoe Blue." The Tahoe Regional Planning Agency was born in 1969. Conservationists defeated plans to build a freeway around the lake, halted construction of more casino districts, ended the practice of dumping sewage in the watershed, and passed a ban on two-stroke watercraft engines. Rochelle Nason led the League to Save Lake Tahoe for eighteen years. During that time, President Bill Clinton in 1997 convened the first Tahoe Summit, which led to a decades-long cleanup effort exceeding $1 billion in cost. At the summit, Washoe leader Brian Wallace negotiated with federal officials for an increased tribal role in land stewardship. Reforms appear to have halted and perhaps even reversed the decades-long trend of reduced water clarity, though climate change and warmer water continue to threaten this progress.

In his inimitable prose, Mark Twain suggested that the lake has the power to bring mummies and skeletons back to life. That remains unproven, but there's no disputing the beauty of the famously blue lake and the majesty of its surrounding mountains. About that, Twain's words still ring true.

VISITOR INFORMATION

Main roads leading into the Lake Tahoe basin stay open year-round unless heavy snowfall or other conditions force their closure. I-80 and Highways 50, 89, 267, and 431 all climb 1,000 feet (or more) higher than Lake Tahoe's elevation of 6,225 feet, and will require chains or all-wheel drive during winter storms.

There are per-person fees for Desolation Wilderness permits for overnight travel. The maximum group size is twelve people. The wilderness also requires permits for day hikes, but they are offered at popular trailheads for no cost.

Sno-Park passes are required to park in several popular areas around Lake Tahoe between November 1 and May 30. One is the nearest trailhead to Castle Peak. A day-use or per-season fee is charged, but these passes are not sold at the unstaffed parking areas. Some local retailers may offer them, but the surest move is to get yours in advance at www.ohv.parks.ca.gov/snoparks.

1. LOVERS LEAP

Lovers Leap shows an impressive and steep rock face to those beneath it, but the trail to its summit is surprisingly mild. An easier hike provides a good experience for beginners, families, and anyone who enjoys a scenic outing.

Distance: 2.8 miles round-trip (all on trails)
Time: 2 hours
Difficulty: Class 1; easy
Parking: Camp Sacramento hikers' lot

Trailhead elevation: 6,400 feet
Summit elevation: 6,944 feet
Elevation gain: 544 feet
Best season: May–Nov
Permits: None needed

FINDING THE TRAILHEAD

 Turn toward Camp Sacramento from Highway 50, across the road from Ralston Peak trailhead and about 3 miles east of Strawberry. There's parking available for hikers and a posted trail map just past the bridge on the left. GPS: N38 48.201' / W120 07.066'

CLIMBING THE MOUNTAIN

Walk through the camp on the westbound road; trail signs point in the right direction. At the edge of camp beside cabins 52 and 53, the signed trail leads to the west. Stay right and westbound as the path briefly joins Sayles Canyon Trail, and then left when the trails part again a short distance later. Through the trees to your right, look for Pyramid Peak and Horsetail Falls in the distance.

At first the trail parallels the South Fork of the American River, but then contours above it and leads left of a large rock formation. You might think this is the summit, but it's not, so simply stay on trail as you pass it. Continue as the path climbs steeply through a forest of oaks and pines to the actual apex of Lovers Leap. Enjoy your view of Eldorado National Forest.

SIERRA SECRETS

Lovers Leap makes a fine winter outing for cross-country skiers and snowshoers.

Nearby Strawberry Lodge has sheltered and fed passersby since 1858. Rock climbers began scaling the formation's abundant granite in the 1950s. Noted free solo climber Alex Honnold made his first ropeless ascents here.

For a closer view of Horsetail Falls, hike from Pyramid Creek Trailhead, about a mile west on Highway 50.

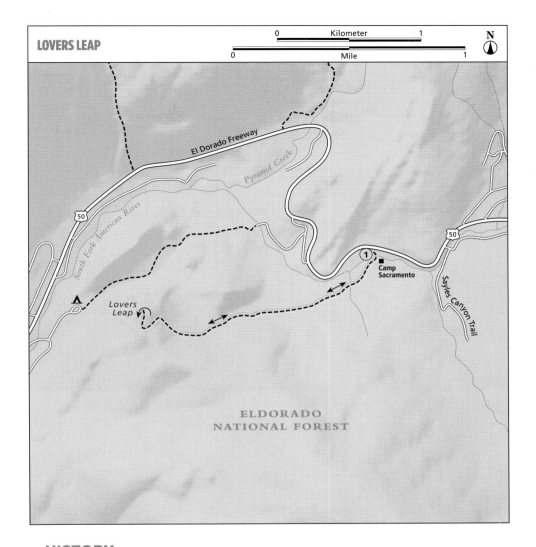

HISTORY

Dozens of peaks across the United States share the name of Lovers Leap. Various legends and tall tales indicate that romantic tragedies occurred on them, but no actual proof of any lovers leaping from their summits has surfaced yet. The Pony Express delivered mail through the river canyon neighboring this Lovers Leap in 1860–1861.

MILES AND DIRECTIONS

0.0 Start at Camp Sacramento and hike west on a road through camp that leads to a path

0.2 Hike west from camp's edge onto signed trail near cabins 52 and 53

0.4 Stay right (west) as the path joins Sayles Canyon Trail

Horsetail Falls gushes north of the trail.

0.5 Stay left (west) as the path splits with Sayles Canyon Trail

1.4 Summit

2.8 Arrive back at the trailhead

2. MARTIS PEAK

Martis Peak boasts one of the best views of Lake Tahoe anywhere, and the easy trek on forest roads to reach it provides good experiences for hikers, cyclists, cross-country skiers, and snowshoers. A historic fire lookout near the summit makes an excellent lunch spot.

Distance: 8 miles round-trip (on forest roads and trails)
Time: 3 to 5 hours
Difficulty: Class 1; easy
Parking: Beside Martis Peak Road

Trailhead elevation: 7,000 feet
Summit elevation: 8,742 feet
Elevation gain: 1,742 feet
Best season: June–Nov
Permits: None needed

FINDING THE TRAILHEAD

Take Highway 267 between Truckee and Kings Beach. Find Martis Peak Road north of the highway, either 8 miles from the signed Placer County line if eastbound, or 0.5 mile from Brockway Summit if westbound. When the gate is closed in winter, you can park in the turnout area near the turnoff. If it's open, you can drive closer to the mountain if you want and park in numerous spaces beside Martis Peak Road. GPS: N39 16.036' / W 120 04.464'

CLIMBING THE MOUNTAIN

During summer months, visitors can park as close as a half-mile from the fire lookout, but let's assume you want more of a workout than that and start at the lower gate. Follow the paved road leading east. Stay on it as you pass several turnoffs to the left and right. Make sure to turn left (north) when you reach an intersection at 1.3 miles, and left again at 3.2 miles. You will see numerous signs for Sierra Pacific Industries asking you to steer clear of its logging operations here.

The road is nearly as easy to follow in winter as in summer; blue trail markers affixed to trees are visible in the uphill and downhill directions. Traveling through a dense forest of pines and firs, you won't see much beyond the trees until you arrive at your destination. Once you reach the upper gate, that's just a half-mile away.

SIERRA SECRETS

Frank "Waddles" Maher (nicknamed for his rolling gait) staffed the lookout for thirty summers in its early years. He posted a sign labeling the shelter "Hotel de Chipmunk" for the legions of rodents that swarmed the hillside, and named some of them after famous visitors to his workplace, like President Teddy Roosevelt and boxer Jack Dempsey. Canned food sustained him, shepherds provided him with goats' milk, and a postman delivered his mail once a month.

There are many ways to include Martis Peak as a destination on other routes, including Tahoe Rim Trail.

Martis Peak

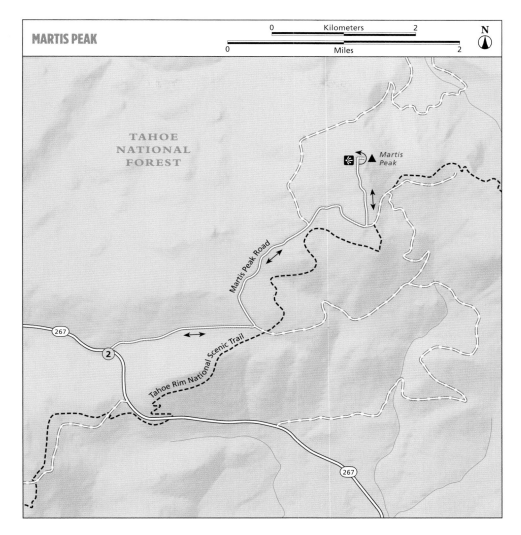

More than a century old, the fire lookout looks over Tahoe National Forest to the southwest and Mount Rose Wilderness to the northeast. But its view of Lake Tahoe itself and the many peaks that crown its southeastern shore will take your breath away and provide the best payoff for your climb. The lookout is open for visitors all year. Look above its windows for drawings and labels identifying the surrounding mountains.

Most visitors declare victory here and descend, as the actual summit looks rather unimpressive and features a view mostly obscured by trees. But if you want to claim it, it's less than 100 feet higher and just 0.2 miles to the southeast.

HISTORY

Martis was the name of a nineteenth-century rancher in these parts; nearby Martis Creek and Martis Valley also take their names from him. The fire lookout atop the mountain was constructed in 1914, vandalized in the early 1990s, and restored in 1997. Today it's

Martis Peak sees a colorful sunrise over Lake Tahoe.

one of the Sierra Nevada's last active fire lookouts; members of California Department of Forestry staff it daily during fire season.

MILES AND DIRECTIONS

0.0 Start at the Martis Peak Road gate and hike, bike, or ski east

1.3 Turn left (north) at intersection, staying on Martis Peak Road

3.2 Turn left (north) at intersection, staying on Martis Peak Road

3.3 At the gate, continue north

3.8 Stop to enjoy the fire lookout, and if you want, continue southeast to the summit

4.0 Summit

8.0 Arrive back at the trailhead

3. **EUREKA PEAK**

Two summits stand above Eureka Lake, but you don't have to choose between them because the same loop trail leads to both. A short and easy ascent, a variety of wildlife, and interesting history combine to make Eureka Peak a rewarding adventure. This is the northernmost mountain in our collection.

Distance: 3.4 miles on a loop (all on trails)
Time: 2 to 3 hours
Difficulty: Class 1–2; easy to moderate
Parking: Eureka Lake lot

Trailhead elevation: 6,184 feet
Summit elevation: 7,447 feet
Elevation gain: 1,263 feet
Best season: May–Nov
Permits: None needed

FINDING THE TRAILHEAD

From the town of Graeagle, take Graeagle-Johnsville Road/County Road A14 southwest and follow signs to Plumas-Eureka State Park. Drive north on County Road 506 past the park museum and through the mountain metropolis of Johnsville for 1.3 miles to Plumas Eureka Ski Bowl parking lot. A dirt road, generally drivable for cars, leads to Eureka Lake. When the gate is closed, hiking to the lake adds 1.7 miles and 700 feet of elevation change each way. GPS: N39 45.815' / W120 42.805'

CLIMBING THE MOUNTAIN

From the lake, a signed trail leads to the southwest and over the dirt-covered dam. Climbing begins through the mountainside forest of jeffrey pines and incense cedars. After 0.8 mile, you'll reach a junction where a signpost directs you left and indicates 1 mile to the summit. Sooner than you might expect, you'll reach the rocky formation you saw from the lake. Make a few Class 2 moves, and you'll stand atop it.

If you then declare victory and descend, you wouldn't be the first to do so. But you actually just summited the North Peak of the mountain. The true summit lies above a forested ridge to the southwest. To reach it, continue clockwise on our figure-six loop trail. In 0.5 mile, you'll reach the boulder pile that appears less impressive than North Peak, but stands 161 feet above it. Either point will show you Sierra Buttes to the south, Lassen Peak to the northwest, and impressive views of the Tahoe and Plumas National Forests all around. Complete the loop to reach the trail junction you passed earlier and retrace your first steps to return to the trailhead.

SIERRA SECRETS

The gate leading to Eureka Lake is open from 8 a.m. to sunset between Memorial Day and Labor Day, conditions permitting. Park officials may extend or shorten its open season, depending on weather.

Keep an eye out for golden eagles, which perch on trees on Eureka Peak.

Eureka Peak

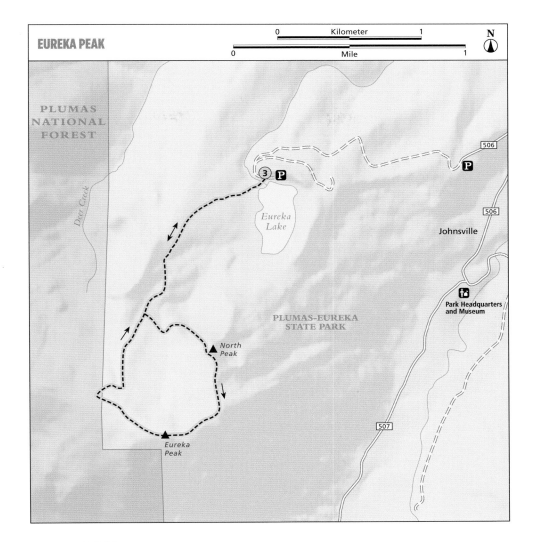

Kilometer

Mile

N

PLUMAS
NATIONAL
FOREST

Deer Creek

506

P

506

Johnsville

3 P

Eureka
Lake

Park Headquarters
and Museum

PLUMAS-EUREKA
STATE PARK

North
Peak

507

Eureka
Peak

HISTORY

After nine miners found gold on the east side of the peak in 1851, prospectors swarmed to the scene, digging more than 60 miles of tunnels and naming the peak "Gold Mountain." They constructed three stamp mills that processed thousands of tons of ore, yielding more than $8 million worth of gold. They also seem to have unintentionally built the world's first ski lift; miners used ore trams to ride up the slopes and skied back down in winter months. The mines closed in 1943.

North Peak attracts many hikers but stands slightly below the true summit.

MILES AND DIRECTIONS

0.0 Start from the Eureka Lake parking area and hike southwest across the dam

0.8 Turn left (southeast) at signed trail junction

1.3 At North Peak, continue hiking south and then west

1.8 At the true summit, continue hiking west and then north

2.0 Turn right (north) at junction and descend

2.6 Stay left (north) at trail junction

3.4 Arrive back at the trailhead

4. MOUNT ROSE

As pretty as its name, and the third-highest peak in the Lake Tahoe area, Mount Rose is easier to summit than Mount Tallac or Freel Peak, but provides a comparably grand adventure and payoff view. This guidebook's only destination in Nevada makes a much better bet than most wagers in the Silver State.

Distance: 10.4 miles round-trip (all on trails)
Time: 5 to 7 hours
Difficulty: Class 1; moderate (for distance and elevation gain)
Parking: Mount Rose Pass lot on Highway 431

Trailhead elevation: 8,900 feet
Summit elevation: 10,776 feet
Elevation gain: 1,876 feet
Best season: May–Oct
Permits: None needed

FINDING THE TRAILHEAD

Park at Mount Rose summit plaza on Highway 431, about 8 miles north of the turn from Highway 28, near Incline Village. Although signs call this area a summit, it is actually a pass. Find the trail's start to the actual summit behind the bathrooms. GPS: N39 18.772' / W119 53.828'

CLIMBING THE MOUNTAIN

Your path starts on a few stairs and then contours northeast of Tamarack Peak on Tahoe Rim Trail for about 2.5 miles. Mount Rose will dominate your view and perhaps your thoughts as you approach. A waterfall, Galena Creek Falls, near the end of this segment makes a nice spot for a break and a drink before the steeper climbing begins.

At the first trail junction, turn right toward Mount Rose; a left turn takes a slightly longer route back to the parking area, an option for your return trip. But for now, start the climb in earnest up to the volcanic peak. You'll reach a saddle and another junction at 9,700 feet. Turn right again (unless you want to take the Rim to Reno Trail) for the final segment to the rocky summit.

SIERRA SECRETS

A University of Nevada professor named James Church constructed a weather observation station on Mount Rose in 1904. During the following winter, Church snowshoed to the summit every two weeks to gather data, helping to develop the modern science of snow surveying.

With the highest Sierra Nevada pass open year-round, the Mount Rose summit plaza makes a great destination for cross-country skiing and snowshoeing.

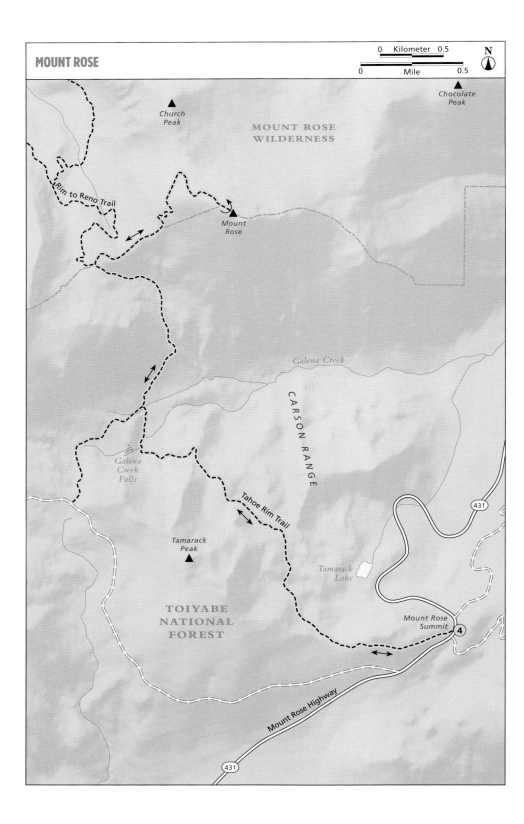

MOUNT ROSE

0   Kilometer   0.5

0   Mile   0.5

N

Chocolate
Peak

Church
Peak

MOUNT ROSE
WILDERNESS

Rim to Reno Trail

Mount
Rose

Galena Creek

C A R S O N   R A N G E

Galena
Creek
Falls

431

Tahoe Rim Trail

Tamarack
Peak

Tamarack
Lake

TOIYABE
NATIONAL
FOREST

Mount Rose
Summit

4

Mount Rose Highway

431

Mount Rose

HISTORY

This peak's name has several competing explanations. Stagecoach driver Hank Monk saw the image of his daughter Rose in the mountain. An 1800s settler named Jacob Rose built a lumber mill in nearby Franktown. And a Washoe City newspaper editor honored Rose Hickman, the first known woman to climb the mountain. No one can say with certainty which of these reasons (if any) correctly explain the moniker, so readers and climbers may draw their own conclusions.

MILES AND DIRECTIONS

0.0 Start at Mount Rose summit plaza and hike west

2.5 Turn right (north) at trail junction

2.7 Turn right (north) at trail junction

3.9 Turn right (northeast) at trail junction

5.2 Summit

10.4 Arrive back at the trailhead

Mount Rose looks down on Humboldt Toiyabe National Forest and Lake Tahoe's north shore.

5. CASTLE PEAK

Easy access, a moderate climb, and excellent scenery explain Castle Peak's popularity in both summer and winter. This peak in Tahoe National Forest is one of the best Sierra Nevada summits that one can drive to reach and then climb on the same day.

Distance: 6 miles round-trip (on dirt road and trails)
Time: 3 to 4 hours
Difficulty: Class 2; moderate (for distance and elevation gain)
Parking: On Castle Peak Road, north of I-80

Trailhead elevation: 7,500 feet
Summit elevation: 9,103 feet
Elevation gain: 1,603 feet
Best season: July–Oct
Permits: None needed

FINDING THE TRAILHEAD

From I-80, take the Castle Peak / Boreal Ridge Road exit and drive north of the freeway onto Castle Peak Road. Park at the end of the road, or beside it. Winter visitors will need to park south of the freeway in the paid Sno-Park area at the end of Bunny Hill Drive. GPS: N39 20.453' / W120 20.856'

CLIMBING THE MOUNTAIN

Our hike begins past the gate on the dirt road in the shade of jeffrey pines and cedars. Take a quick right at a sign showing the cross-country ski route. Hike beside Castle Valley with Castle Peak looming above for about 0.5 mile until the road splits; take the left option heading uphill. Continue until the road ends and turn left onto a path that quickly meets the Pacific Crest Trail. Turn left again and climb about 200 feet to Castle Pass. Here our route turns right, leading to Castle Peak's western ridge, which climbs steeply to the summit.

Three large volcanic formations stand on the summit plateau. The first one hikers encounter is an easy scramble and most people climb atop it, declare victory, and descend. The middle one is steeper. The third and steepest tower to the east marks the true summit. To reach it requires a 50-foot ascent on Class 3 terrain. Experienced rock climbers do this often, but most folks will be happier on the first summit block closest to the western ridge. All three formations afford views of Sierra Buttes, Donner Lake, Mount Judah, and other Tahoe-area summits, plus Lake Tahoe itself.

Andesite Peak, a modest peak to the south, makes a short and worthy detour from Castle Pass; it might be a better primary destination for families with young children.

HISTORY

Members of the Wheeler Survey made the first known ascent in 1877. Members of the Whitney Survey named the peak "Mount Stanford" in 1896. But because Placer County already had a summit by that name, its moniker was changed to Castle Peak, "so named from its conical shape."

Castle Peak

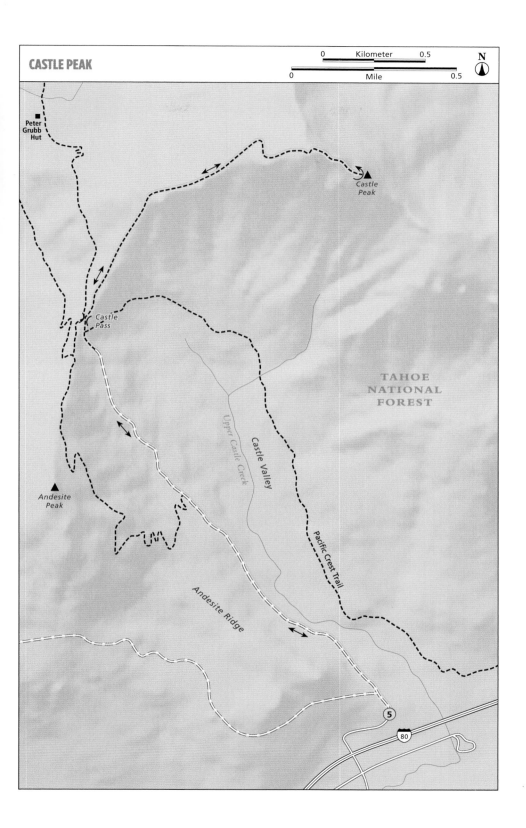

CASTLE PEAK

Peter Grubb Hut

Castle Peak

Castle Pass

TAHOE NATIONAL FOREST

Upper Castle Creek

Castle Valley

Andesite Peak

Pacific Crest Trail

Andesite Ridge

5

80

Kilometer

Mile

N

Castle Peak's southern view includes peaks of Tahoe National Forest.

SIERRA SECRETS

While snow will cover the road, skiers and snowshoers will normally find a well-beaten path to Castle Pass and into Round Valley, to the Sierra Club's Peter Grubb Hut, a fine overnight destination for those with reservations. The name honors a young mountaineer and Sierra Club member who died of unknown causes on a European cycling trip in 1937.

MILES AND DIRECTIONS

0.0   Start from the end of Castle Peak Road and hike north onto the dirt road, past the gate

0.5   Turn left (northwest) at road split

1.5   As the road ends, take the path leading northwest

1.6   Turn left (northwest) as the path meets the Pacific Crest Trail

1.7   Turn right (north) onto Castle Peak Trail

3.0   Summit

6.0   Arrive back at the trailhead

6. SIERRA BUTTES

If you pass through Sierra City, you can't help but notice the impressive Sierra Buttes towering over the town. Hiking to their highest summit is far easier than it looks from below, but climbing the steep and exposed stairs to the fire lookout will test your courage!

Distance: 4.6 miles round-trip (on dirt roads and trails)
Time: 2 to 4 hours
Difficulty: Class 1; moderate (for distance and elevation gain)
Parking: Sierra Buttes trailhead

Trailhead elevation: 7,000 feet
Summit elevation: 8,587 feet
Elevation gain: 1,587 feet
Best season: June–Oct
Permits: None needed

FINDING THE TRAILHEAD

From Highway 49 about 5 miles east of Sierra City, turn onto Gold Lake Highway and drive about 1.4 miles. Turn left over a bridge and onto Sardine Lake/Packer Lake Road. Then 0.2 mile later, turn right onto Packer Lake Road. Continue past a turnoff for Packer Lake on FR 621 as our road becomes steep, winding and narrow (but paved). Some 4.5 miles past the bridge, turn left at a split onto Butcher Ranch Road. Pavement now gives way to a dirt road. Follow signs to a trailhead and parking area for Sierra Buttes and Pacific Crest Trail. GPS: N39 36.700' / W120 39.924'

CLIMBING THE MOUNTAIN

Before we begin, let's have a word about dogs. Our furry friends are legal on this trail, and most will do fine on the hike. But climbing the exposed stairs to the lookout station can greatly frighten them, so this dog-loving author recommends leaving them behind.

Our hike starts on a southbound dirt road overlapping the Pacific Crest Trail (PCT), climbing through cedars and pines. After 0.5 mile the dirt road branches left, but our route lies right and becomes a footpath up a ridge. The grand views that soon appear merely hint at what's to come.

Turn left at the next trail junction to leave the PCT and climb steeply up switchbacks on the shortest route to the glacier-carved summit. A boulder field marks a detour to the left, revealing lakes below. A second detour on a short dirt path appears next, with better views of more lakes. The main trail climbs above the tree line and joins a jeep road that ascends more switchbacks to the top. The fire lookout is no longer active, but the balcony around it is open to the public. Views of the Lake Basin area are worth the bold climb up the 176 stairs, so summon your courage!

HISTORY

Maidu and other Native American groups spent summers in this area. Miners established nearby Sierra City in 1850, and prospectors dug dozens of mines. The fire lookout opened in 1915. Five forest employees built the heart-pounding stairs to the lookout in 1964.

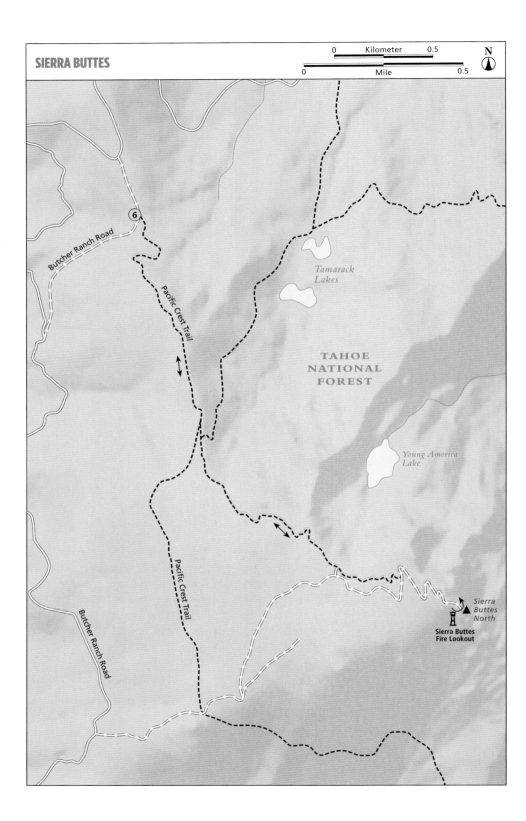

SIERRA BUTTES

Butcher Ranch Road

6

Pacific Crest Trail

Tamarack Lakes

TAHOE
NATIONAL
FOREST

Young America Lake

Pacific Crest Trail

Butcher Ranch Road

Sierra
Buttes
North

Sierra Buttes
Fire Lookout

Sierra Buttes

MILES AND DIRECTIONS

0.0   Hike south from Pacific Crest Trail and Sierra Buttes trailhead

0.5   Turn right (south) at junction, staying on PCT

0.8   Turn left (southeast) at trail junction, leaving PCT

1.1   Turn left (southeast) at trail junction

1.9   Turn left (north) as trail meets dirt road

2.3   Summit

4.6   Arrive back at the trailhead

SIERRA SECRETS

The Sierra Buttes Mines produced some $17 million worth of gold. Five prospectors unearthed a 109.2-pound gold nugget, the largest in California history, here in 1869. The mines closed in 1937, although tales of gold continue to draw miners and tourists to Plumas County at the northern end of the Mother Lode.

There are good free, undeveloped campsites available along Gold Lake Highway.

7. **FREEL PEAK**

Climb the highest mountain in the Lake Tahoe area on a trail with fewer hikers than popular rivals Mount Tallac or Mount Rose. Expect a little bit of everything: The route is rocky, grassy, sandy, shady, and sunny at different points. A high-clearance vehicle may be needed to reach the trailhead.

Distance: 9 miles round-trip (all on trails)	**Parking:** That depends; see below
	Trailhead elevation: 8,420 feet
Time: 4 to 6 hours	**Summit elevation:** 10,881 feet
Difficulty: Class 2; moderate to strenuous (for distance and elevation gain)	**Elevation gain:** 2,461 feet
	Best season: July–Oct
	Permits: None needed

FINDING THE TRAILHEAD

From South Lake Tahoe, take Highway 89 southeast. About a mile east of Luther Pass, turn left onto Willow Creek Road (FR 051). From here on, the dirt road may be smooth and accessible, or it could be rough and muddy enough to require a truck; proceed with caution. If conditions permit, drive northeast for about 3.5 miles, crossing two bridges, and then take a left fork toward Horse Meadow. Before you reach the meadow, park in the visible parking area. GPS: N38 49.806' / W119 54.047'

CLIMBING THE MOUNTAIN

Take the trail toward Armstrong Pass, climbing about 0.75 mile to reach it. Then turn right onto the signed Tahoe Rim Trail, hiking north for about 3 miles through a few switchbacks to the saddle below Freel Peak. This segment includes shady forest, tall grass, rocky scenery, and finally, a sandy slope. At the saddle, turn off the northbound rim trail here for the obvious summit spur, which features more sand. The good news is that you're almost there; the view is fantastic, and the sand will make for a fast and easy descent.

SIERRA SECRETS

Freel Peak occupies the highest point in El Dorado County.

From the summit, climbers can see the neighboring Jobs Peak and Jobs Sister. Early maps referred to the three peaks as "Job's Group of Mountains," honoring Moses Job, who opened a store in Sheridan, Nevada, in the 1850s. To achieve both Jobs summits from Freel Peak adds about 5 miles to the outing.

Melting snow forms the number "27" on the northwest side of the mountain, facing the lake, each spring.

Freel Peak

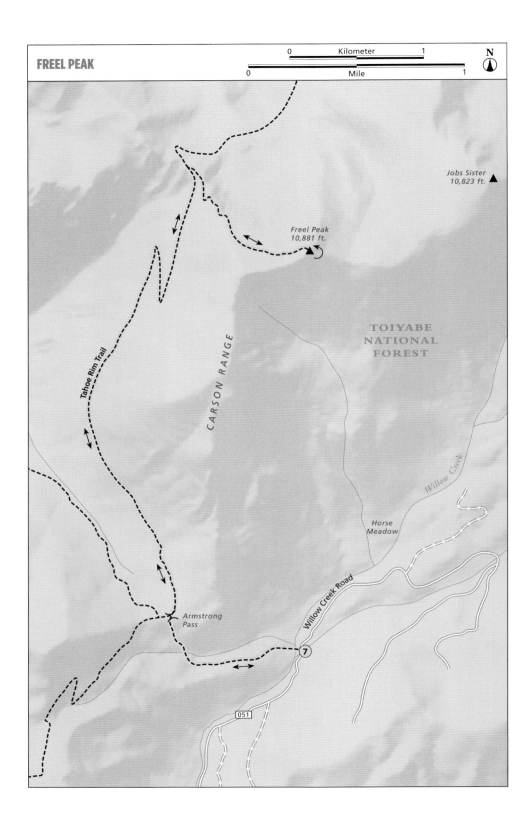

FREEL PEAK

Kilometer

Mile

N

Jobs Sister
10,823 ft.

Freel Peak
10,881 ft.

Tahoe Rim Trail

CARSON RANGE

TOIYABE
NATIONAL
FOREST

Willow Creek

*Horse
Meadow*

Willow Creek Road

Armstrong
Pass

7

051

HISTORY

Members of the US Coast Survey made the first recorded ascent on September 15, 1874. Surveyor William Eimbeck named the peak for miner and rancher James Freel, who settled at the foot of the mountain in the late 1800s. Previously some had called it "Sand Mountain" because of its sandy summit, or "Bald Mountain."

MILES AND DIRECTIONS

0.0 Start from parking area nearest Armstrong Pass and hike west on Armstrong Pass Trail

0.75 Turn right (north) at Armstrong Pass onto Tahoe Rim Trail, which leads past the mountain's west slope

3.75 Turn right (southeast) at junction onto summit trail and climb steeply up switchbacks

4.5 Summit

9.0 Arrive back at the trailhead

Freel Peak's summit puts hikers in striking distance of Jobs Peak and Jobs Sister.

8. RALSTON PEAK

Though Ralston Peak stands right beside Highway 50, it may qualify as a secret gem because the mountain's flanks obscure its summit from the view of passing motorists. But climbers who achieve the peak will enjoy a commanding view of Desolation Wilderness.

Distance: 6.6 miles round-trip (all on trails)
Time: 3 to 5 hours
Difficulty: Class 2; moderate to strenuous (for distance and elevation gain)

Parking: Ralston Peak trailhead lot
Trailhead elevation: 6,400 feet
Summit elevation: 9,235 feet
Elevation gain: 2,835 feet
Best season: June–Nov
Permits: Required

FINDING THE TRAILHEAD

 Park beside Highway 50 at the Ralston Peak trailhead lot, across the road from Camp Sacramento and about 3 miles east of Strawberry. GPS: N38 48.238' / W120 07.048'

CLIMBING THE MOUNTAIN

A trail sign points the way on a dirt road that climbs uphill and curves to the left. You'll find the self-issue permit station in about 200 yards; write yourself a free permit to enter Desolation Wilderness.

Our hike continues with a steady climb through the pine and oak forest above neighboring Tamarack Creek. A Desolation Wilderness boundary sign appears after about 1.4 miles. Soon the trail climbs switchbacks above the tree line, and the wooded forest gives way to shrubs, grass, and granite as the mountaintop comes into view.

Near the summit, the route splits and climbers have a choice of trails. Turn right for a shorter (0.7 mile) and steeper final push, and left for a longer (1.4 miles) and more gradual option.

Enjoy your view that includes Pyramid Peak to the west, Round Top far to the south, Echo Lakes to the east, and Lake Tahoe to the north. Altogether that's quite a payoff for a fairly short hike!

> ### SIERRA SECRETS
>
> Many enjoy this outing during winter months with cross-country skis, snowshoes, or just hiking boots, but familiarity with the route helps when snow obscures the trail.
>
> Abundant wildflowers on this hike typically peak in July.
>
> Equestrian alert: The Forest Service allows horses on this trail.

HISTORY

This mountain's name apparently honors William Chapman Ralston (1828–1875), a native of Ohio who came to California in 1850. "Billy" Ralston worked in San Francisco

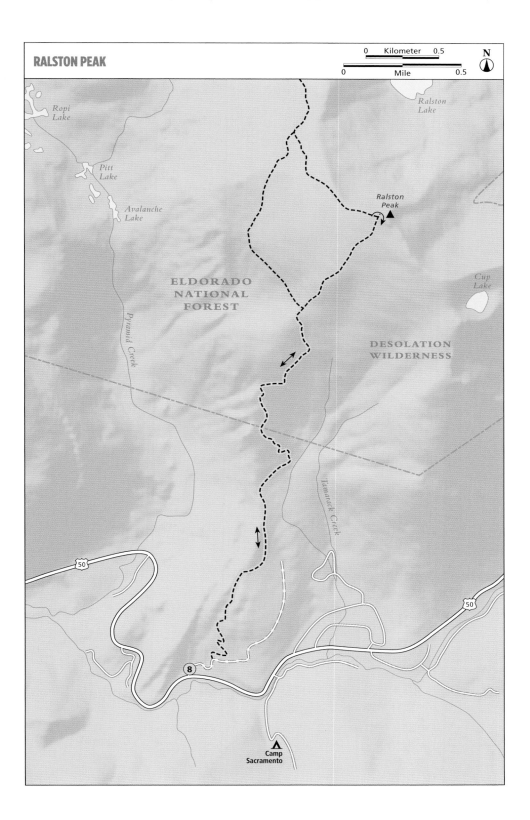

Ropi
Lake

Pitt
Lake

Avalanche
Lake

Ralston
Lake

Ralston
Peak

ELDORADO
NATIONAL
FOREST

Cup
Lake

Pyramid Creek

DESOLATION
WILDERNESS

Tamarack Creek

50

50

8

Camp
Sacramento

0   Kilometer   0.5

0   Mile   0.5

N

as a steamship agent, later becoming a banker and hotel developer before drowning while swimming in the bay. The Wheeler Survey used Ralston's name on its 1881 map.

MILES AND DIRECTIONS

0.0 Park beside Highway 50 at Ralston Peak trailhead and hike northeast on the dirt road

0.2 Leave dirt road, get a free permit at the trail sign, and take trail leading north

1.0 Stay left (north) at trail junction

2.6 Turn right (northeast) for shorter, steeper option

3.3 Summit

6.6 Arrive back at the trailhead

9. MOUNT TALLAC

The most prominent peak in the Tahoe basin provides the best view of the lake and perhaps the best adventure in the area. Despite a thigh-burning climb, it attracts thousands of climbers each year.

Distance: 9.6 miles round-trip (all on trails)
Time: 6 to 8 hours
Difficulty: Class 2; strenuous (for distance and elevation gain)
Parking: Mount Tallac trailhead lot

Trailhead elevation: 6,480 feet
Summit elevation: 9,735 feet
Elevation gain: 3,255 feet
Best season: June–Oct
Permits: Required

FINDING THE TRAILHEAD

From South Lake Tahoe, take Highway 89 northwest from the Highway 50 junction and drive 3.9 miles toward Emerald Bay. Turn left onto Mount Tallac Road (a forest sign for Camp Concord and Camp Shelly marks the turnoff, which is straight across the highway from Baldwin Beach Road) and drive about a mile to the parking area and trailhead. GPS: N38 55.288' / W120 04.107'

CLIMBING THE MOUNTAIN

Get a self-issued permit at the trailhead to enter Desolation Wilderness. Start the hike through the forest as the trail begins to climb. Fallen Leaf Lake comes into view as you climb up and along a sharp ridge in about 0.5 mile. The wilderness boundary and Floating Island Lake follow within the next mile. Enjoy the shade of the forest's pines, cedars, and oaks while you can because you're about to climb into a realm of rock, sun, and wind. Stay right as a side trail leads left and steeply down to Fallen Leaf Lake. Continue south to Cathedral Lake. This is the last reliable source of water, and you're going to need plenty of it before the climb is over.

There are four trail junctions between Cathedral Lake and the summit, some offering variations that also lead to the summit, but the simplest approach is to simply turn right at all four going up (and left at all four going down). Our path veers west through Cathedral Basin as we climb above the tree line. Here the route becomes steep and leads

> **SIERRA SECRETS**
>
> Snowfields cover the path in places early in the season, requiring careful footing and route finding. Be careful following the footprints of earlier hikers through snow because they sometimes lead off the trail.
>
> This hike becomes uncomfortably hot, dusty, and crowded in the summer months; consider an early start.
>
> Rough, rocky trail on the upper half of this route makes hiking poles especially helpful.

Mount Tallac

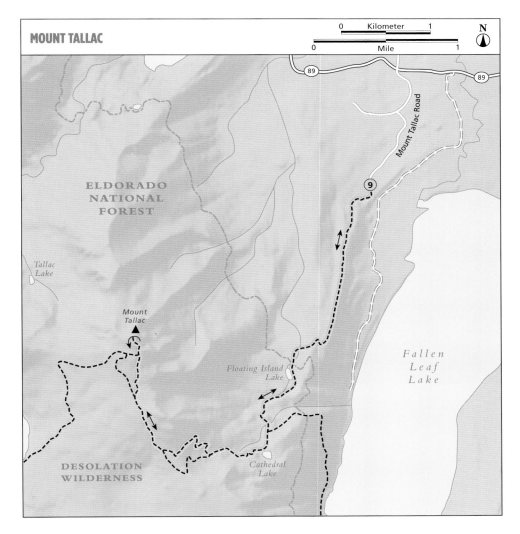

over a large talus slope. After gaining a ridge, the climbing eases as the path turns north and leads through scattered trees on the mountain's south slope.

As you take the final steps, you will reach a perch overlooking magnificent Lake Tahoe. Hang onto your hat in the wind, find a good sitting rock, and take some time to enjoy the peerless view before descending.

HISTORY

Whitney Survey maps labeled the mountain as "Crystal Peak." But the Washoe called it *Talah-act*, meaning "big mountain," and members of the Wheeler Survey adapted the name as "Tallac" in 1877. A snow cross appears on the northeast face. Legends predicted that when it melts, it forebodes a heavy winter, war, or even the end of the world.

Desolation Wilderness fills the western view from Mount Tallac.

MILES AND DIRECTIONS

0.0 Start at Mount Tallac Road parking lot, get a free permit at the self-issue station, and hike south on the trail

2.4 Stay right (south) at junction with trail to Fallen Leaf Lake

3.1 Turn right (north) at trail junction

3.8 Turn right (northwest) at trail junction

4.3 Turn right (north) at trail junction

4.6 Turn right (north) at trail junction

4.8 Summit

9.6 Arrive back at the trailhead

10. PYRAMID PEAK

A steep hike leads through densely forested Rocky Canyon. Then, above the tree line, Pyramid Peak comes into view and climbers ascend its south ridge. Large boulders and talus mark the final approach to the highest point and best view in Desolation Wilderness. This tough 4,000-foot climb will test your resolve!

Distance: 7 miles round-trip (all on trails)
Time: 5 to 7 hours
Difficulty: Class 2; strenuous (for elevation gain)
Parking: Beside Highway 50, 1 mile east of Strawberry

Trailhead elevation: 5,908 feet
Summit: 9,984 feet
Elevation gain: 4,080 feet
Best season: June–Oct
Permits: Required

FINDING THE TRAILHEAD

Park on the shoulder of Highway 50 about a mile east of Strawberry or about 0.7 mile west of Pyramid Creek Trailhead. The trailhead is unmarked, but look for an electronic road sign facing eastbound traffic. Just east of the sign, a creek flows beneath the highway and an eastbound passing lane begins. From here, look north for a rocky slope with a fallen log visible above it. Rocky Canyon Trail starts there and becomes visible as soon as you climb the slope to the log. GPS: N38 48.503′ / W120 08.156′

CLIMBING THE MOUNTAIN

Although this hike starts in Eldorado National Forest, it soon enters Desolation Wilderness, where even day hikes require permits, and this trailhead has no self-issue permit station. But there is one at the nearby Ralston Peak trailhead on Highway 50, across the road from Camp Sacramento.

Steep, demanding climbing begins immediately. Take your time! The path ascends through a thick forest of pines, oaks, and manzanita, over fallen logs and beside a creek. The trail is rugged but fairly easy to follow, and there are rock cairns along the way to keep you on route. Eventually the trees thin out, and the trail curves northwest, and then north, as Pyramid Peak appears in the distance. Ascend the obvious ridge up scree and talus. Near the summit, you must negotiate large boulders.

HISTORY

W. W. Harvey named the peak in 1862. William Brewer (1828–1910) of the Whitney Survey achieved the first recorded ascent on August 20, 1863. The botanist climbed alone, as "no one was inclined to accompany me, all dreading the labor," and wrote that "it was all climb, but not so hard as I had expected." Brewer described the view as "the grandest in this part of the Sierra."

Pyramid Peak

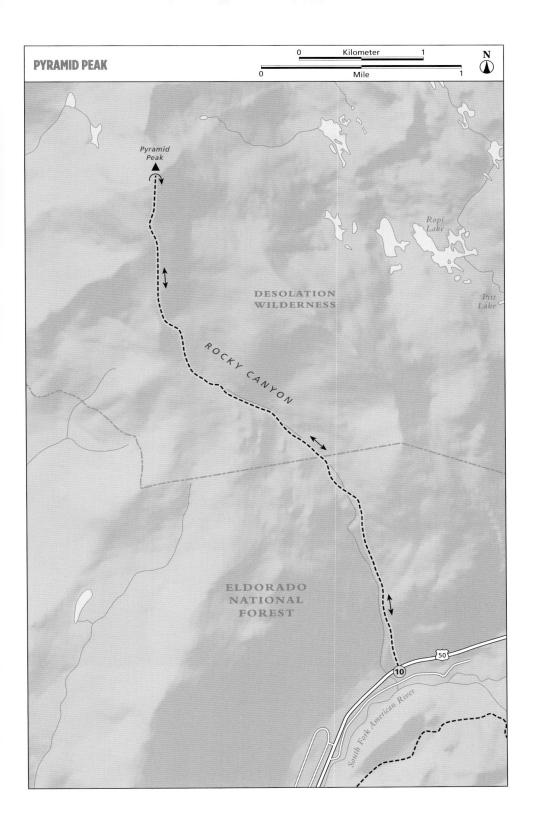

PYRAMID PEAK

0   Kilometer   1
0   Mile   1

N

Pyramid
Peak

Ropi
Lake

DESOLATION
WILDERNESS

Pitt
Lake

ROCKY CANYON

ELDORADO
NATIONAL
FOREST

50

10

South Fork American River

Lake Aloha borders the mountain's northeast base.

MILES AND DIRECTIONS

0.0 Park beside Highway 50 about 1 mile east of Strawberry, find unsigned Rocky Canyon Trail north of the road near the electronic road sign, and hike north

1.2 As the trail enters Desolation Wilderness, continue north

3.5 Summit

7.0 Arrive back at the trailhead

SIERRA SECRETS

Rocky Canyon Trail is not an official Forest Service path and does not appear on most maps.

For more variety, make a loop by starting or finishing at Pyramid Creek trail-head, about 0.75 mile east of the Rocky Canyon trailhead. Hike up Horsetail Falls Trail until it ends in about 1.5 miles. Then scramble off-trail left of the falls up to the ridge where Pyramid Peak comes into view. This route is slightly longer and includes third-class terrain. If that sounds like too much trouble, then the walk up to see Horsetail Falls alone is an easy and scenic option. There is a fee to park at Pyramid Creek trailhead.

BONUS PEAKS NEAR LAKE TAHOE

ANGORA PEAK

Elevation: 8,588 feet   **Difficulty:** Moderate

This mountain beside Angora Lakes (named for a breed of sheep that grazed near here) provides a quick though steep climb in a pretty, lesser-known area. Take Angora Ridge Road (east of Fallen Leaf Lake) until it ends in a parking lot (there is a parking fee). Hike southwest to the Angora Lakes. Angora Peak stands northwest of the upper lake. You may find use trails leading up it, or you could make your own line. To gain the summit requires ascending Class 2 or Class 3 terrain, depending on your route. This 2- or 3-mile climb gains about 1,250 feet and takes one or two hours. Conditions are best from June through October.

MOUNT JUDAH

Elevation: 8,243 feet   **Difficulty:** Moderate

A loop trail takes hikers atop a mountain named for Theodore Judah, who surveyed the nearby railroad route in the 1850s. Locate Donner Peak trailhead on Old Donner Summit Road and hike south on the Pacific Crest Trail. Climb switchbacks to the junction where the loop begins. Turn left (north) for the clockwise ascent to the top, which turns east and then passes just a few hundred yards from the summit of Donner Peak, a fun detour. Curve south for another mile to Mount Judah's summit. Finish the clockwise loop for a 4.8-mile trek, or return the way you came. The hike gains 1,200 feet of elevation and takes about three hours. Conditions are best from June through October.

ANDERSON PEAK

Elevation: 8,683 feet   **Difficulty:** Strenuous

This adventure begins like the Mount Judah climb but leads several miles deeper into Tahoe National Forest. Locate Donner Peak Trailhead on Old Donner Summit Road and hike south on the Pacific Crest Trail. Climb to a trail junction and turn right (south) to stay on the PCT. Hike south past Mount Judah and Mount Lincoln to the base of Anderson Peak. The PCT leads around the mountain in a counterclockwise direction. The gentlest summit approach leads up the southeast ridge. Winter travelers use the Sierra Club's Benson Hut, which stands below the mountain's north face; some take the Sugar Bowl ski lift onto Mount Lincoln to reduce distance and elevation gain. Otherwise, the 14-mile round-trip gains 1,600 feet, taking six to ten hours. Conditions are best from June through October.

Giant sequoias bathe in morning light at Calaveras Big Trees State Park.

CENTRAL SIERRA

When trapper Jedediah Smith and two companions attempted the first crossing of the Sierra Nevada range by European Americans in May of 1827, they struggled to find their way through the rugged mountains and nearly froze to death in a fierce spring snowstorm.

"During the night the storm increased in violence and the weather became extremely cold," Smith wrote. "We were uncertain how far the mountains extended to the east. The wind was continually changing and the snow drifting and flying in every direction . . . It seemed that we were marked out for destruction and that the sun of another day might never rise to us. But He that rules the Storms willed it otherwise and the sun of the 27th rose clear upon the gleaming peaks."

Although three of their animals perished, Smith and his party survived, later cresting the range near Ebbetts Pass.

Today visitors in the Central Sierra still find rougher travel and fewer people than those in Lake Tahoe and Yosemite encounter. But the remote mountains neighboring Carson Pass, Ebbetts Pass, and Sonora Pass reward climbers with unique adventures. And while modern-day explorers will surely discover their own challenges, they will also benefit from much that early travelers like Smith lacked, such as roads, maps, weather forecasts, and guidebooks like *Sierra Summits*.

GEOLOGY

Volcanoes and erosion played key roles in shaping the Central Sierra mountains, which have abundant igneous and metamorphic rock. Before plate movement caused the Sierra Nevada range to rise, volcanoes erupted and expelled thick layers of lava. Then the range's rise displaced the hardened lava before glaciers and streams eroded it into interesting formations. The results are visible on and around mountain summits throughout the Central Sierra area.

For example, Round Top near Carson Pass is an inactive volcanic vent that probably supplied much of the area's large amounts of volcanic rock. The neighboring Elephants Back is a lava dome. Near Sonora Pass, the erosion of lava formed mountains like the Dardanelles, Sonora Peak, and Leavitt Peak. But the erosion of quartz that revealed gold proved far more interesting to the thousands of prospectors who arrived starting in 1849.

HISTORY

Tribes including the Miwok, Washoe, Mono, and Paiute inhabited the Central Sierra area prior to the arrival of European Americans, moving up and down the mountains with the seasons. Archaeological and historical evidence of their settlements remain in places

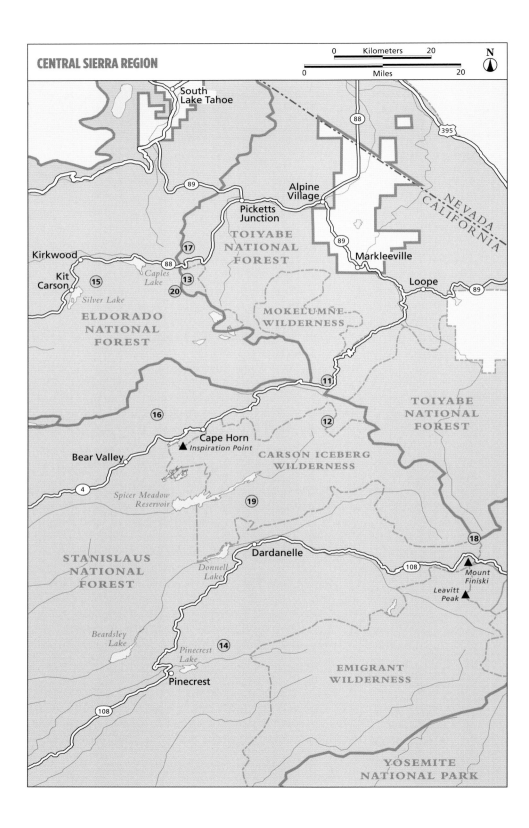

like Indian Grinding Rock State Historic Park in Amador County, and some of their descendants still live in the region.

Smith was far from the last newcomer to make a difficult crossing. Against the advice of Washoe leaders, John Fremont's expedition headed west over the mountains in the winter of 1844. After five weeks of toil and danger, the party reached the safety of Sutter's Fort, and their route over Carson Pass now carries the name of their guide, Kit Carson.

The discovery of gold near Coloma in 1848 brought a wave of eager miners known as "49ers" starting in 1849, forever changing the Sierra Nevada mountains and the lives of the people who lived there. Many European Americans made their way to the western foothills by way of Carson Pass. Ebbetts Pass and Sonora Pass saw established routes and travelers by the 1850s as well. Chinese Americans flocked to the gold country, too, mostly crossing the Pacific and arriving in San Francisco. Some 300,000 people in all raced to California, which became a state in 1850.

However, prospectors' lust for gold and disregard for Native Americans led to years of atrocities, a steep decline in the Native population, and the loss of most tribal homes. In addition, the heavy-handed mining techniques employed left lasting scars on the land that are still visible today.

Cities, including Auburn, Placerville, Angels Camp, Columbia, and Sonora, sprouted near productive mines. The populations of many towns plummeted after the Gold Rush died out around 1855, but the region still draws tourists to experience its historic atmosphere today. For example, Railtown 1897 State Historic Park near Jamestown gives visitors rides on a steam locomotive that once supported logging.

Outdoor recreation supports this area's economy as well. Kirkwood attracts skiers to its resort on Highway 88. Nature lovers enjoy the giant sequoias at Calaveras Big Trees State Park on Highway 4. Anglers frequent popular fishing holes like New Melones Lake, Spicer Meadow Reservoir, and Silver Lake. Congress designated Mokelumne Wilderness in 1964, Emigrant Wilderness in 1975, and Carson-Iceberg Wilderness in 1984. Though some here still make a living in mining and logging, tourism and recreation appear to provide the most promising economic future for Central Sierra communities.

Significant people of the Central Sierra include John Marshall and John Sutter, whose discovery set off the Gold Rush. William Perkins of Tuolumne County wrote *Three Years in California*, a fascinating journal of the era. Author Bret Harte wrote his popular short story "The Luck of Roaring Camp" in 1868, after living in Amador County. Other Gold Rush figures who later achieved prominence include John Studebaker, founder of the automobile company; Domingo Ghirardelli, founder of the chocolate company; future US senator George Hearst (father of the newspaper titan); and Leland Stanford, the future governor and founder of Stanford University.

John "Snowshoe" Thompson carried the mail over the snow-covered range multiple times each winter from 1856 to 1876. Lola

Lupine frames a summit in Mokelumne Wilderness.

A statue of a miner by sculptor Ken Fox greets visitors to Auburn and commemorates the Gold Rush.

Montez, a well-known actress, dancer, and once the mistress to King Ludwig I of Bavaria, lived in the Gold Country from 1853 to 1855. While there, she met and encouraged the young Lotta Crabtree, who became a widely known actress and comedian known as "The Nation's Darling" during a forty-year career. More than three decades before women won the vote nationwide, Tuolumne County elected Rose Morgan, its first elected woman, who served as county superintendent of schools in 1886.

William Fuller, a Miwuk chief, helped to establish a reservation now named Tuolumne Rancheria in 1907. Leann Donner App, the last survivor from the doomed Donner Party expedition of 1846, lived in Jamestown until her death in 1930. Bud Klein and Dick Reuter established Kirkwood ski resort in 1972. Mildred Filiberti won election as Tuolumne County's first woman supervisor in 1976. Noted attorney Melvin Belli was born and buried in Sonora.

Conservationists, including George Wendt and Marty McDonnell, fought to protect the Stanislaus, Tuolumne, and Clavey Rivers. Conrad Anker established scores of first ascents in Yosemite and elsewhere, summiting Mount Everest three times. Angels Camp chose Amanda Folendorf, just thirty-one, as the nation's first female deaf mayor, and Tuolumne County hired Tracie Riggs as its first female county administrator in 2018.

And though he was no native to these parts, Mark Twain brought unending attention and tourism to the area with his classic short story, "The Celebrated Jumping Frog of Calaveras County." In so doing, the author made the Central Sierra a bit less mysterious and foreboding than the wilderness Smith, Fremont, and Carson found.

VISITOR INFORMATION

Carson Pass on Highway 88 remains open year-round, conditions permitting, though drivers will need chains and/or four-wheel drive during and after storms. With an apex of 8,574 feet, Highway 88 is the highest trans-Sierra road that remains open to motorists in winter.

Ebbetts Pass on Highway 4 and Sonora Pass on Highway 108 are typically open between May and November, but opening and closing dates vary based on weather and road conditions.

Eldorado National Forest has a ranger station on Highway 88 in Pioneer and an information station at Carson Pass. Stanislaus National Forest has visitor centers on Highways 4 and 108.

11. EBBETTS PEAK

This short and easy ascent makes a nice outing for those traveling Highway 4 over Ebbetts Pass, and might be the best mountain in this book for introducing children to the rewards and adventure of climbing.

Distance: 1 mile round-trip (all on trails)
Time: 1 hour
Difficulty: Class 1; easy
Parking: Beside Highway 4 at Ebbetts Pass

Trailhead elevation: 8,736 feet
Summit elevation: 9,160 feet
Elevation gain: 424 feet
Best season: June–Oct
Permits: None needed

FINDING THE TRAILHEAD

Park beside Highway 4 at Ebbetts Pass, or about a 0.5 mile east of the pass in a dirt lot southeast of the highway. GPS: N38 32.671' / W119 48.705'

CLIMBING THE MOUNTAIN

Find the dirt road leading northwest from the pass. Follow it about 0.25 mile to its end. Take the northbound trail up to the saddle and then climb a use trail northeast up the last few hundred feet to the summit.

For variety, descend northwest toward Sherrold Lake, where you'll meet the Pacific Crest Trail. Turn right to take it back to Highway 4, where another right returns you to Ebbetts Pass in a few hundred yards. Making this loop adds only 0.5 mile to the total distance. Be cautious of this option in the early season when the north slope of Ebbetts Peak will have snowfields.

SIERRA SECRETS

Ebbetts Peak and the Ebbetts Pass area normally have snow for a few weeks after Highway 4 reopens, often in May, with fun opportunities for cross-country skiers and snowshoers. In fact, John "Snowshoe" Thompson delivered mail through this area on his cross-country skis from 1856 to 1876.

Despite John Ebbetts's vision, no railroad was ever constructed here, though a toll road opened in 1862 to accommodate silver mining in the Eastern Sierra. The road became public and free to use in 1911.

HISTORY

Miwuk and Washoe Indians traveled the Ebbetts Pass corridor, as did cartographer Jedediah Smith in 1827, and pioneer John Ebbetts in 1851. Ebbetts later suggested the route for a transcontinental railroad to surveyor George Goddard. After Ebbetts died in a steamboat explosion in 1854, Goddard named the pass after him.

Ebbetts Peak

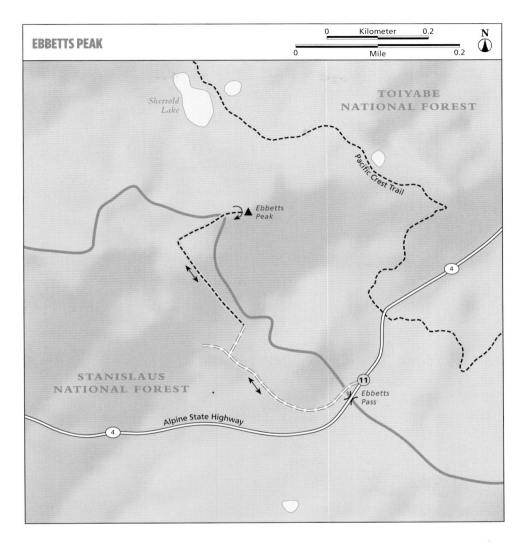

MILES AND DIRECTIONS

0.0 Start from Ebbetts Pass and hike northwest on a forest road to its end

0.25 Hike north on a trail to the saddle west of the summit

0.4 Take a use trail leading right (east) to the summit

0.5 Summit

1.0 Arrive back at the trailhead

12. **FOLGER PEAK**

A short and pretty hike in Stanislaus National Forest takes hikers to a modest summit suitable for beginners, kids, and dogs. This climb gives you a good reason to get off the main highway and discover the attractive Highland Lakes area.

Distance: 2 miles round-trip (all on trails and use trails)
Time: 1 to 2 hours
Difficulty: Class 1; easy
Parking: Beside Highland Lakes Campground

Trailhead elevation: 8,620 feet
Summit elevation: 9,720 feet
Elevation gain: 1,100 feet
Best season: June–Nov
Permits: None needed

FINDING THE TRAILHEAD

Take Highland Lakes Road leading southeast from Highway 4, about 4 miles east from Hermit Valley Campground if eastbound, or 1.3 miles west of Ebbetts Pass if westbound. Drive on the partly paved, partly dirt road for 5.8 miles to Highland Lakes Campground, beside the second (and smaller) lake. The road can be rough, narrow, and winding in places, but is generally drivable for cars without high clearance. GPS: N38 29.364' / W119 48.469'

CLIMBING THE MOUNTAIN

Walk through the campground area on the west side of the road and locate site #4. The use trail leads from it through lodgepole pines to the west. Soon you'll emerge from the trees, turn north, and start steeper climbing up a gravelly slope. When you reach the secondary peak on the mountain's southern flank, you've gained about 75 percent of the climb's elevation. The last segment is slightly steeper and rockier than the lower portion, but still Class 1 if you stay on-route.

Our summit view features peaks of Mokelumne and Carson-Iceberg Wildernesses and 9,795-foot Hiram Peak to the southeast. If Folger Peak warmed you up for a bigger challenge, that could be your nightcap. After descending, find Hiram's trailhead across the road in the east side

SIERRA SECRETS

Highland Lakes Road opens later than Highway 4, so check with the Forest Service if you're considering a trip in the early season.

The Folger brothers published the first newspapers in the Eastern Sierra, and "were well respected for their patriotism and defense of ethical journalism," according to author Gena Philibert-Ortega.

Though just a stone's throw apart, the two Highland Lakes are headwaters for two different watersheds. The northeastern lake flows into the Mokelumne River drainage; the southwestern one flows into the Stanislaus River drainage.

Highland Lakes offers brook trout fishing and camping for a fee (charged per night).

Folger Peak

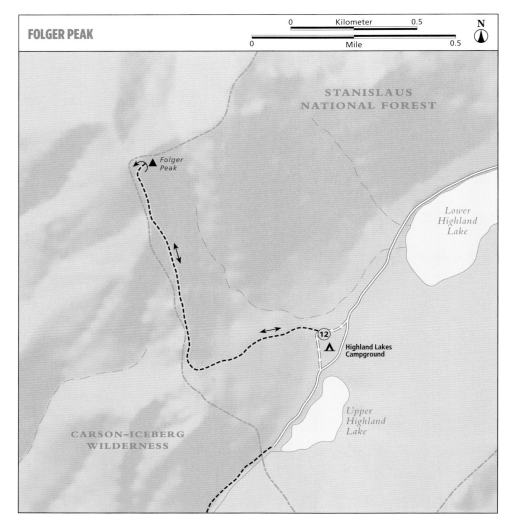

of the campground, starting in site #31. The 1.5-mile use trail to the summit involves steeper climbing and Class 2 terrain.

While practically inaccessible in winter, Folger Peak may hold enough snow for skiers to make a few turns after the road opens in late spring or early summer.

HISTORY

This mountain carries the name of an Eastern Sierra newspaper pioneer, although no one knows for sure which one. Robert Folger (1820–1899) founded the *Alpine Chronicle* in 1864 and was the West Coast's oldest working journalist at the time of his death. His brother Alexander Folger (1831–1902, and identified as Andrew by some sources) became the town's first postmaster, and also published newspapers with his brother in Markleeville and Bridgeport.

Folger Peak looks down on neighboring Hiram Peak and Airola Peak.

MILES AND DIRECTIONS

0.0 Start at Highland Lakes Campground and hike north from site #4 onto a westbound trail leading to the summit

1.0 Summit

2.0 Arrive back at the trailhead

13. ELEPHANTS BACK

Thanks to a high trailhead, this gentle outing up a volcanic slope that resembles its namesake provides an authentic backcountry feeling within a short distance and time frame. Because Highway 88 is open nearly year-round, this fine climb beckons in all seasons.

Distance: 4 miles round-trip (on trails and cross-country)
Time: 2 to 3 hours
Difficulty: Class 1; easy
Parking: Carson Pass lot

Trailhead elevation: 8,574 feet
Summit elevation: 9,585 feet
Elevation gain: 1,011 feet
Best season: Year-round
Permits: None needed

FINDING THE TRAILHEAD

Park beside Highway 88 at Carson Pass, which charges a parking fee in summer and fall months, and requires a Sno-Park pass (not available on-site) Nov 1–May 30. GPS: N38 41.657' / W119 59.324'

CLIMBING THE MOUNTAIN

Hike south through the woods on the Pacific Crest Trail, reaching Frog Lake in about a mile. From here Elephants Back rises above the horizon and shows its steep northeast face. Don't worry; you're going up the gentler back side.

Turn right at the trail junction toward Winnemucca Lake as you leave the PCT. If you detoured to Frog Lake, be careful not to miss the junction just south of it, or else you're on your way to Mexico. Continue south as you pass the mountain on your left. There's no summit trail, so turn toward it as you reach its mild southwest face, picking your own line up the loose volcanic rock. Once you reach the summit ridge, climb north to the high point.

Rewarding your effort is a sweeping view of Round Top, The Sisters, Red Lake Peak, Carson Pass, and a vast portion of Mokelumne Wilderness (which straddles the Stanislaus, Eldorado, and Humboldt-Toiyabe National Forests).

HISTORY

Mountain surveyor George Goddard called this long, ridge-like summit "the Elephant" in 1855. An Alpine County map referred to it as "Elephant Mountain" in 1870. Members of the Wheeler Survey dubbed it "Elephants Back" in 1877.

SIERRA SECRETS

You might meet PCT thru-hikers resting on the porch of the Carson Pass information center.

If the Carson Pass lot is full, you may find space in the Meiss trailhead lot just to the west. For a longer hike, start at Woods Lake Trailhead a few miles west of Carson Pass (for both options, the parking fee still applies).

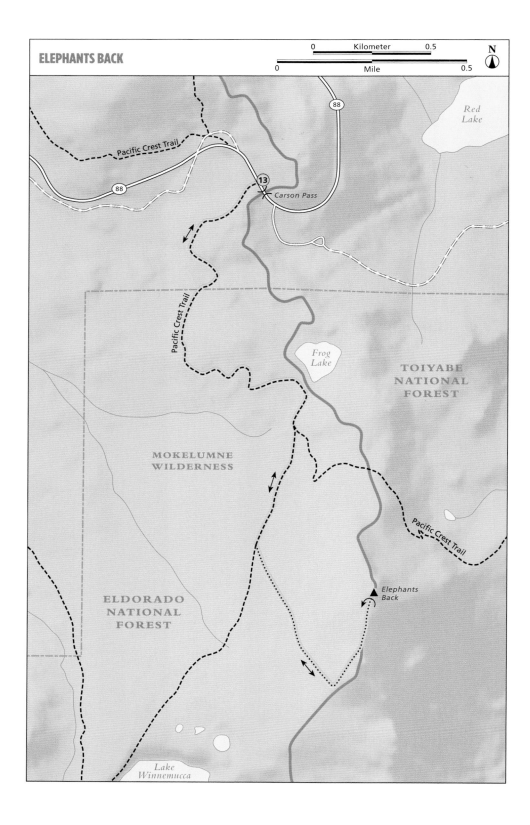

ELEPHANTS BACK

0   Kilometer   0.5

0   Mile   0.5

N

Red Lake

Pacific Crest Trail

88

88

13

Carson Pass

Pacific Crest Trail

Frog Lake

TOIYABE NATIONAL FOREST

MOKELUMNE WILDERNESS

Pacific Crest Trail

ELDORADO NATIONAL FOREST

Elephants Back

Lake Winnemucca

MILES AND DIRECTIONS

0.0 Start at Carson Pass, hiking south on the PCT

1.0 At Frog Lake, stay right (south)

1.1 At a trail junction stay right (south), leaving the PCT

1.6 Turn left (east) off the trail and ascend cross-country to the mountain's southwest ridge

1.8 Turn left (north) and climb toward the summit

2.0 Summit

4.0 Arrive back at the trailhead

Sam the climbing canine revels in the scenery of Carson Pass.

14. PINECREST PEAK

While many recreate in popular Pinecrest Lake, few hike or bike to the summit of its namesake mountain to the northeast. A scenic and moderate outing on Pinecrest Peak will make you better appreciate your swim in the lake's cool blue waters.

Distance: 9.6 miles round-trip (on trails and forest roads)
Time: 4 to 6 hours
Difficulty: Class 1; moderate (for distance and elevation gain)
Parking: Dirt lot on FR 4N27

Trailhead elevation: 6,500 feet
Summit elevation: 8,440 feet
Elevation gain: 1,940 feet
Best season: May–Nov
Permits: None needed

FINDING THE TRAILHEAD

Drive east on Highway 108 about 2.5 miles past Strawberry. Turn right onto Herring Creek Road / FR 4N12. Drive east for 2.8 miles and then turn right onto FR 4N27, a dirt road, but normally a passable one for low-clearance vehicles. After another 1.3 miles, park where the road ends. GPS: N38 13.292' / W119 57.496'

CLIMBING THE MOUNTAIN

Cross the bridge over Herring Creek. Stay left at first junction with a "PCP" sign. Make a sharp left at the second junction with a "peak" sign. The trail climbs and soon reaches a small pond. To the right is a clearing overlooking Pinecrest Lake and the Stanislaus River, which is worth a brief stop to appreciate.

Now our route climbs switchbacks on the southwest flank of Pinecrest Peak. During the ascent, climbers will pass a second overlook marked with a "view" sign, another good spot for a breather. On the upper section, the trail becomes rough and crosses granite slabs, but cairns mark the way and it's not overly difficult to follow.

SIERRA SECRETS

Do this climb early in the season before the gate on Herring Creek Road opens to allow motor vehicles on high forest roads.

For a longer hike of about 12 miles, begin at Pinecrest Lake. Hike clockwise over the dam and along the northern shore. Look for a signed side trail to Catfish Lake. From here, proceed east and up on a trail that connects with the route from FR 4N27.

Cyclists can reach the summit by riding on FR 4N12 to FR 5N31. This intersects with our hiking route for the final segments on FR 5N55Y and FR 5N55YB. From the gate at the end of Herring Creek Road's pavement to the summit is about 5.5 miles, or an 11-mile round-trip. Bikers could also make a 15-mile loop by descending the hiking trail toward the dirt lot at the end of FR 4N27; this segment is open to cyclists in the downhill direction only. Your author found it rough riding, and recommends the out-and-back forest roads option instead. Cyclists may use the high forest roads before they open to motor vehicles.

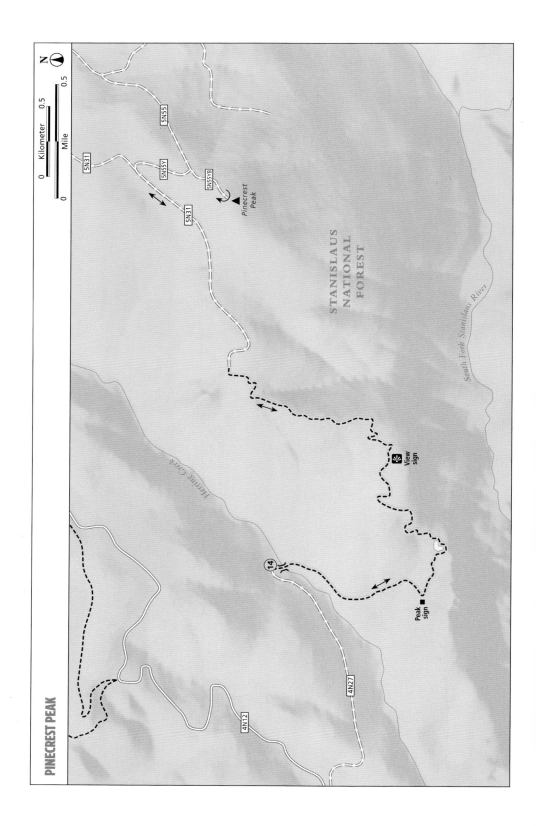

PINECREST PEAK

N

0   Kilometer   0.5

0   Mile   0.5

5N55

5N31

5N55Y

5N55YB

5N31

Pinecrest
Peak

STANISLAUS
NATIONAL
FOREST

South Fork Stanislaus River

Herring Creek

View
sign

14

Peak
sign

4N12

4N27

Climbing eases at a rocky plateau. Here are remains of the lookout station that stood here until fire destroyed it. Pick up FR 5N31, leading northeast. The rounded top of Pinecrest Peak comes into view on your right. After 1.2 miles on the road, turn right onto FR 5N55Y for a short distance, and then turn right again onto FR 5N55YB, which takes you the final steps to the broad summit. Enjoy your view of the Emigrant and Carson–Iceberg Wildernesses.

HISTORY

Developers built the first Strawberry Dam in 1856 and the second in 1916, allowing the South Fork of the Stanislaus River to form Strawberry Lake. The reservoir provides water to foothill communities that sprang up in support of logging after the Gold Rush. Residents changed the name to Pinecrest Lake in the 1960s. An observation station stood on a rocky plateau near Pinecrest Peak from 1939 to 1973.

MILES AND DIRECTIONS

0.0   Hike south past gate and across bridge over Herring Creek

0.7   Turn left (east) onto trail at peak sign

1.0   Hike past pond and climb trail to northeast

Pinecrest Peak's summit trail passes above the South Fork of the Stanislaus River.

1.8   Continue climbing past view sign

3.0   At lookout station ruins, pick up FR 5N31 leading northeast

4.2   Turn right (south) onto FR 5N55Y

4.5   Turn right (southwest) onto FR 5N55YB

4.8   Summit

9.6   Arrive back at the trailhead

15. THUNDER MOUNTAIN

Thunder Mountain beckons Kirkwood skiers, Silver Lake anglers, and all who drive past it on Highway 88. This easily accessible trail in Eldorado National Forest takes hikers past interesting rock formations, and to a summit boasting a fine view of Silver Lake and beyond.

Distance: 7.2 miles round-trip (all on trails)
Time: 3 to 5 hours
Difficulty: Class 1; moderate (for distance)
Parking: Thunder Mountain trailhead lot

Trailhead elevation: 7,950 feet
Summit: 9,410 feet
Elevation gain: 1,460 feet
Best season: June–Oct
Permits: None needed

FINDING THE TRAILHEAD

Find the signed Thunder Mountain trailhead south of Highway 88 between Silver Lake and Kirkwood. A dirt lot provides ample parking. GPS: N38 42.338' / W120 06.452'

CLIMBING THE MOUNTAIN

Follow the well-marked trail south and east through the forest, climbing to Carson Spur, the first overview and rock formation. Continue above the tree line south to the Two Sentinels, more lava formations that mark the way and pique curiosity.

Next, hikers will climb beside (but not atop) Martin Point as they continue south on volcanic slopes toward the summit. Along the way, look for wildflowers, including woolly mule's ears, dwarf phlox, and butterballs.

Near the top the trail splits and summit-bound hikers should stay to the right. From the junction a spur trail continues another 0.5 mile to the summit and, a short distance beyond that, its western peak.

HISTORY

US Forest Service personnel chose this name because "thunderheads appear to build up in that area." In the 1860s, Zachary Kirkwood purchased the nearby land that became a town carrying his name. Kirkwood ski resort opened in 1972.

SIERRA SECRETS

Thunder Mountain marks the highest point in Amador County.

Those wishing a longer outing can make a loop around the entire mountain. From the junction near the summit, take the southeast-bound trail (a left turn for those approaching from the trailhead). This descends to Horse Creek Trail, which leads westward beneath the mountain's lava wall that faces Silver Lake. Hikers will later have to cross the highway twice to finish the loop and return to Thunder Mountain trailhead. This option extends the hike to 12.3 miles.

Thunder Mountain

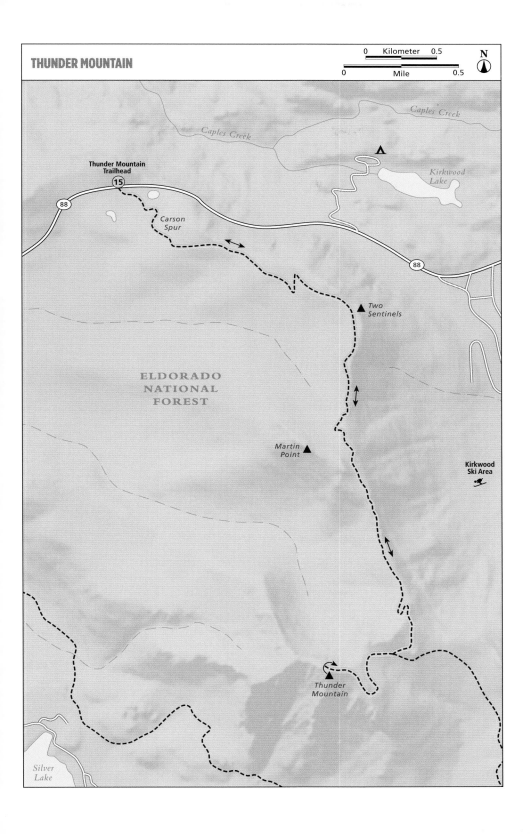

THUNDER MOUNTAIN

0 Kilometer 0.5
0 Mile 0.5

N

Caples Creek

Caples Creek

Thunder Mountain
Trailhead

15

88

Carson
Spur

Kirkwood
Lake

Two
Sentinels

ELDORADO
NATIONAL
FOREST

Martin
Point

Kirkwood
Ski Area

88

Thunder
Mountain

Silver
Lake

Silver Lake highlights the summit's western view.

MILES AND DIRECTIONS

0.0 Start at Thunder Mountain trailhead and hike southeast on Thunder Mountain Trail

1.5 Stay right at junction to stay on Thunder Mountain Trail

3.1 Stay right at junction onto spur trail

3.6 Summit

7.2 Arrive back at the trailhead

16. MOUNT REBA

This simple outing from Highway 4 in Stanislaus National Forest follows a jeep road almost to the summit, providing a fun route for hikers, a steep but doable ride for mountain bikers, and a worthy trek for cross-country skiers and snowshoers.

Distance: 6 miles round-trip (all on forest roads)
Time: 3 to 5 hours
Difficulty: Class 1; moderate (for distance)
Parking: Round Valley Sno-Park lot beside Highway 207

Trailhead elevation: 7,700 feet
Summit elevation: 8,842 feet
Elevation gain: 1,142 feet
Best season: June–Oct
Permits: None needed

FINDING THE TRAILHEAD

Find a parking area beside Highway 207 / Mount Reba Road, marked on some maps as Round Valley Sno-Park. If eastbound on Highway 4, drive about 2 miles from the village of Bear Valley and turn left; if westbound, drive about 1 mile from Lake Alpine and turn right. Once on Highway 207, the parking area is within 0.2 mile on the right. A Sno-Park permit is required to park here Nov 1–May 30. GPS: N38 29.096' / W120 01.196'

CLIMBING THE MOUNTAIN

Take FR 7N93 northbound from the lot, climbing up switchbacks and quickly gaining elevation in Mokelumne Wilderness. Some maps identify this route as a jeep trail. Winter trekkers take note: Snow will likely cover both the sign and the road. Climbing eases for a while and then steepens again as we gain the summit ridge. Turn left to continue another mile toward the summit. On the way, enjoy the woolly mule's ears and other wildflowers that abound in season.

The road ends atop a summit-like plateau that's 8,842 feet high, and this is good enough for most people; however, US Geological Survey (USGS) maps identify a slightly lower point 0.7 mile west as the summit of Mount Reba. How can that be the true summit if it's 87 feet shorter than the plateau? It's not far away, so you might as well go and place your conquest of the mountain beyond dispute. Look for a use trail that leads to the scattered rock formations. Both summits boast fine views of the Mokelumne River canyon and Mokelumne Peak to the west and the Dardanelles to the south.

HISTORY

Harvey Blood, who developed and operated a toll road through this area, named the mountain in 1875 for his only daughter. Workers on the road also thought highly of Reba Blood, who was known for baking and delivering pies to them. Nearby Mount Reba Ski Bowl opened in 1967, and changed its name to Bear Valley in 1991.

Mount Reba

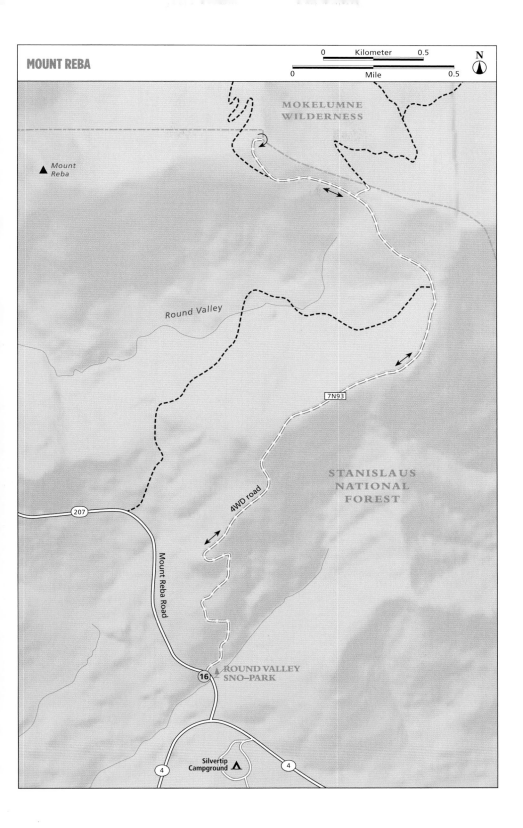

N

0   Kilometer   0.5

0   Mile   0.5

MOKELUMNE
WILDERNESS

▲ Mount
   Reba

Round Valley

7N93

STANISLAUS
NATIONAL
FOREST

207

4WD road

Mount Reba Road

16   ▲ ROUND VALLEY
       SNO–PARK

4   Silvertip
     Campground ⛺   4

MILES AND DIRECTIONS

0.0 Start at the trailhead, hiking north and climbing quickly on FR 7N93

2.0 At road junction, turn left (west) to continue toward the summit

3.0 Summit

6.0 Arrive back at the trailhead

Mount Reba's southern view features peaks of Stanislaus National Forest.

17. RED LAKE PEAK

Starting close to Carson Pass, this climb leads up a steep but simple trail to the most easily reached peak of at least 10,000 feet in this collection. A few Class 3 moves take climbers atop the summit rocks, but it's not necessary to scale them in order to enjoy the fine panoramic view; the rest of the ascent is Class 1. Highway 88 provides access all year (except during and after heavy storms).

Distance: 3 miles round-trip (all on trails)
Time: 2 to 3 hours
Difficulty: Class 3; moderate (for elevation gain and scrambling at summit)

Parking: Meiss trailhead lot
Trailhead elevation: 8,574 feet
Summit elevation: 10,063 feet
Elevation gain: 1,489 feet
Best season: June–Oct
Permits: None needed

FINDING THE TRAILHEAD

Park beside Highway 88 at Meiss trailhead or in the nearby Carson Pass lot. Both sites charge a parking fee in summer and fall months, and require a Sno-Park pass (not available on-site) Nov 1–May 30. GPS: N38 41.817' / W119 59.491'

CLIMBING THE MOUNTAIN

Find an unsigned trail leading north from the Meiss parking area, just west of the out-houses. Do not take the northbound Pacific Crest Trail like most other hikers here do. Instead, climb north through the picturesque junipers. Soon the trail clears the tree line. Climb steadily to a saddle where the incline briefly eases. Then the ascent resumes as the path nearly traces the border between Eldorado and Humboldt–Toiyabe National Forests.

A secondary summit will fill your view as you ascend the next segment; don't be discouraged to reach it and see the true summit beyond! The remaining climb is only about 400 feet. Now with our goal in sight, stay on the trail as it turns northeast and up the mountain's southwest flank. A simple slope leads from the shoulder to the southernmost summit, which is good enough for most people. To reach the true summit, follow a use trail that leads counterclockwise around the peak. A variety of Class 3 options lead up the east side of the volcanic rock.

SIERRA SECRETS

Fremont's 1844 expedition struggled to reach Fort Sumter, losing more than half its livestock and resorting to eating mules and dogs. But all the men survived, and Fremont named the pass in honor of Kit Carson, who led them to safety.

Red Lake Peak overlooks Meiss Meadow to the northwest. There the German immigrant Meiss family built a cabin and barn in the 1870s and spent summers there well into the twentieth century. The historic buildings still stand on land the Forest Service acquired in 1965.

Red Lake Peak

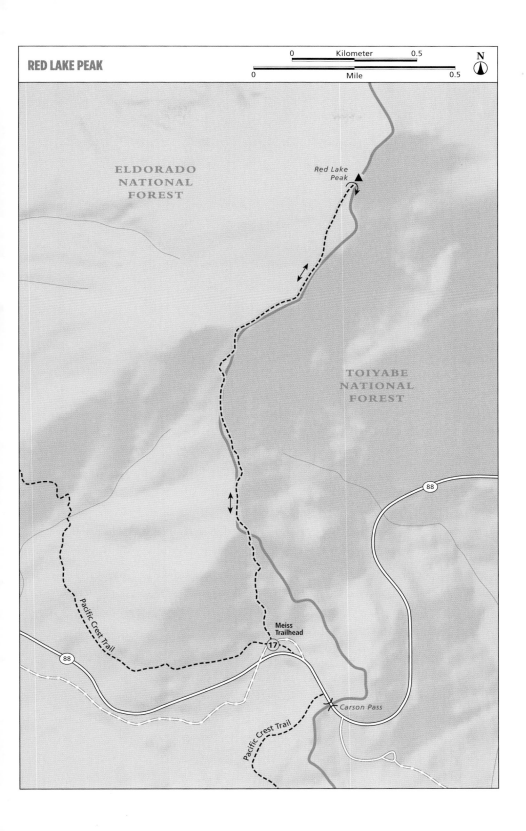

ELDORADO
NATIONAL
FOREST

Red Lake
Peak

TOIYABE
NATIONAL
FOREST

88

Pacific Crest Trail

Meiss
Trailhead

17

88

Carson Pass

Pacific Crest Trail

Red Lake Peak's view includes Meiss Meadow.

Our summit view includes Red Lake, Elephants Back, and Round Top to the south; Meiss Meadow and Meiss Lake to the northwest; and the distant peaks of Desolation Wilderness to the north.

Red Lake Peak makes a fine winter adventure, too. While snow covers the trail described above, skiers and snowshoers have to plot their own paths. Skiers will especially enjoy the descent, which features glorious and gentle turns back to the road.

HISTORY

This summit has a unique and little-known historical distinction. When John Fremont's expedition made a bold winter crossing of what's now called Carson Pass in 1844, he and Charles Preuss ascended the peak on February 14. This became the first documented mountain climb in the Sierra Nevada range. The peak carried the name "Red Mountain" on an 1864 map, but took on its current name, after nearby Red Lake, by 1891.

MILES AND DIRECTIONS

0.0   Hike north on an unsigned trail (not the PCT) from Meiss trailhead

1.5   Summit

3.0   Arrive back at the trailhead

18. SONORA PEAK

Reasons abound to climb volcanic Sonora Peak: an easy approach, a short climb, a high summit, and an incredible payoff view. If you pass anywhere near Sonora Pass in summer or fall, the outing almost becomes a must-do. Unlike most summits, this one has a loop variation that adds variety without much additional distance.

Distance: 5 miles round-trip (all on trails)
Time: 2 to 3 hours
Difficulty: Class 2; moderate (for elevation gain)
Parking: Beside Highway 108 at Saint Marys Pass trailhead

Trailhead elevation: 9,432 feet
Summit elevation: 11,459 feet
Elevation gain: 2,027 feet
Best season: June–Oct
Permits: None needed

FINDING THE TRAILHEAD

 Park in a dirt lot at Saint Marys Pass trailhead, located north of Highway 108 about 0.8 mile west of Sonora Pass. A trailhead sign is visible beside the parking area. There's also a pullout on the south side of the road. GPS: N38 20.227' / W119 38.732'

CLIMBING THE MOUNTAIN

Our path starts as a dirt road and soon becomes a single-track trail. Hike steadily up to Saint Marys Pass, soon climbing above the tree line. From here on, a few scattered pines, low-growing sagebrush, occasional snowfields, and wildflowers in season will be your traveling companions. The trail may be a little hard to spot in places, but just head north to the saddle, keeping the mountain on your right.

At the saddle, you'll find a wilderness boundary sign and a four-way junction. Our route leads east as the climbing continues up a hill to a wide plateau of red volcanic rock and soil. Now you're looking right at the summit. If snow covers the trail, aim for the northwest ridge, where the route climbs the last 500 feet. At the summit, you can rest beside a rocky windbreak while perusing the register. Nearby mountains in clear view include Leavitt Peak, Night Cap Peak, and Stanislaus Peak.

Return on the same route, or for more variety, descend the use trail along southeast ridge to connect with the Pacific Crest Trail. Turn right at the PCT junction to return to Sonora Pass, and then follow the road west to your parking area. Making this loop will increase the total distance of your hike to about 6.5 miles.

HISTORY

This mountain takes its name from the Gold Rush town to the southwest, which was named by miners from the Mexican state of Sonora. Westbound emigrants of the Clark-Skidmore Party of Ohio and Indiana made the first documented crossing of Sonora Pass in 1852, though Miwuk and Paiute Indians traveled and traded across this passage

Sonora Peak

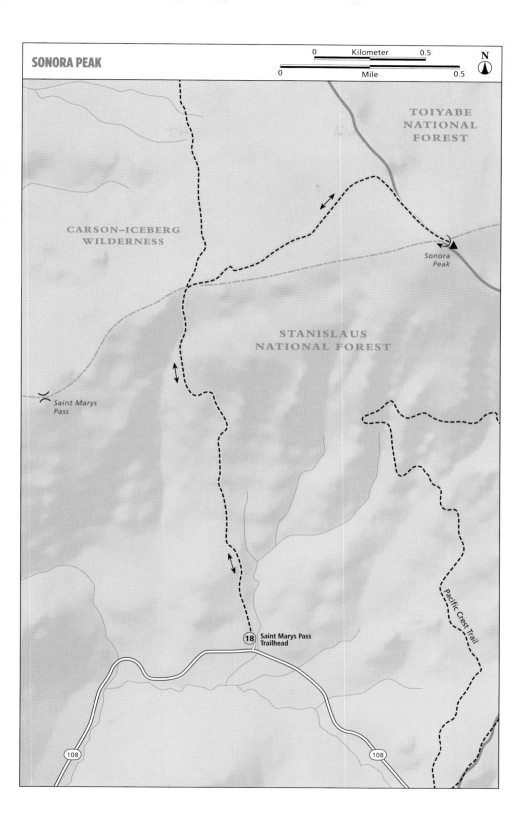

Sonora Peak affords a look deep into the mountainous Emigrant Wilderness.

far earlier. Members of the Wheeler Survey, which arrived in 1877, apparently named the peak.

> ### SIERRA SECRETS
>
> Sonora Peak marks the highest point in Alpine County and also straddles Mono County.
>
> Snow typically still covers this mountain and the surrounding area when Sonora Pass reopens after each winter, normally in May. Great cross-country skiing, snowshoeing, and snow play usually abound for a few weeks after the road opens.

MILES AND DIRECTIONS

0.0 Start at Saint Marys Pass trailhead and hike north on a dirt road that soon becomes a single-track trail

1.2 Turn right (east) at Saint Marys Pass toward the mountain's northwest ridge

2.0 Ascend switchbacks up the northwest ridge as the trail turns southeast to the summit

2.5 Summit

5.0 Arrive back at the trailhead

19. DARDANELLES WEST

Though this summit appears distant and unreachable from Highway 108 vistas, a forest road leads high up its shoulder and within a few miles of its summit. A well-traveled trail leads to the base of the mountain; from there, climbers must navigate and scramble to reach the summit. For those wishing to try their skills on a seldom-attempted and undeveloped mountain, Dardanelles West provides a good learning opportunity.

Distance: 4 miles round-trip (on-trail and cross-country)
Time: 3 to 5 hours
Difficulty: Class 2 to 3; strenuous (for off-trail scrambling)
Parking: Sword Lake trailhead

Trailhead elevation: 7,150 feet
Summit elevation: 8,834 feet
Elevation gain: 1,684 feet
Best season: June–Oct
Permits: None needed

FINDING THE TRAILHEAD

From Highway 108, turn left onto Clark Fork Road (about 3 miles east of Donnell Vista, or 3 miles west of the village of Dardanelle). After crossing the bridge, turn left onto FR 6N06. The road goes from well paved to roughly paved to dirt as you pass a winter gate. Road conditions vary from year to year; some low-clearance cars make the journey, but a high-clearance and/or four-wheel-drive vehicle is preferable. Continue about 6 miles to the road's end and Sword Lake trailhead. GPS: N38 22.678' / W119 55.535'

CLIMBING THE MOUNTAIN

From the posted sign at the parking area, start on the trail toward Sword Lake, but quickly turn right off the main route after about 50 feet. Though unsigned, the trail leading northeast is clear. You will reach a wilderness boundary sign within about ten minutes, and then find two large logs (one bigger than the other) lying directly across the trail in about ten more minutes. Although the mountain is not visible through the trees at this point, you can begin ascending here. You can also continue hiking until the peaks come into view on your left, though that will add additional distance.

As you climb above the majority of trees, the mountaintops will become visible. The rounded eastern peak is the true summit, and it's also the easiest to reach if you choose your path well. Avoid large swaths of manzanita and other growth. Navigate around steep rock formations. Although there is no established route, you may find footsteps and faint use trails. Ascending a creek bed is an option. The eastern summit has a lightning rod atop it and views of Spicer Meadow Reservoir, the other nearby Dardanelles peaks, and Carson-Iceberg and Emigrant Wildernesses.

HISTORY

The name "Dardanells" appears on a Sonora Pass map from 1853. Settlers apparently named the three neighboring peaks for their resemblance to The Dardanelles strait

Dardanelles West

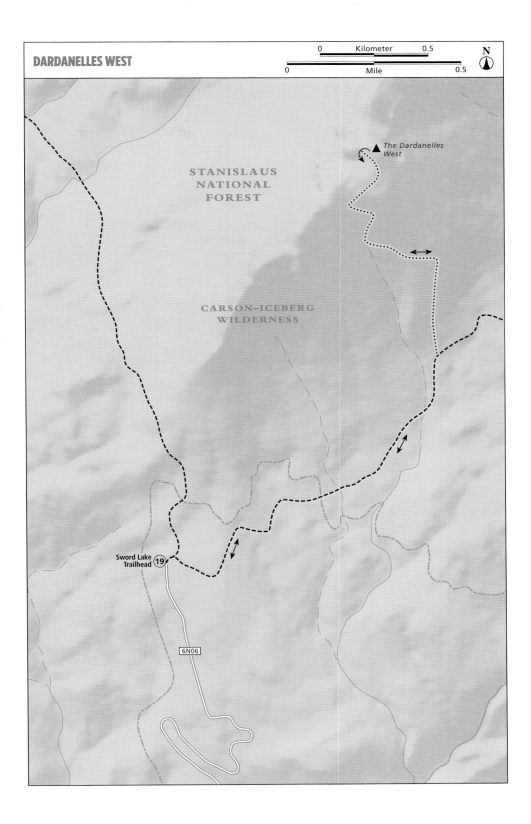

The Dardanelles
West

STANISLAUS
NATIONAL
FOREST

CARSON–ICEBERG
WILDERNESS

Sword Lake
Trailhead (19)

6N06

0   Kilometer   0.5

0   Mile   0.5

N

Dardanelles West stands above Spicer Meadow Reservoir.

between the Aegean Sea and the Sea of Marmara, separating Asian and European Turkey. Today the name also applies to a small community and a campground on Highway 108.

MILES AND DIRECTIONS

0.0 Start from Sword Lake trailhead, hiking north, but after just 50 feet, turn right (northeast) onto an unsigned but clear pack trail

1.0 Turn left (north) off the pack trail and traverse up the southwest slope of the mountain

2.0 Summit

4.0 Arrive back at the trailhead

SIERRA SECRETS

Our trail to Dardanelles West also leads toward Dardanelles Cone, slightly higher, at 9,524 feet.

Lava flow from about ten million years ago followed by centuries of erosion created the tall volcanic formations now known as the Dardanelles.

This hike passes through both Tuolumne and Alpine Counties.

For a good picture of the Dardanelles summits, visit Donnell Vista on Highway 108.

20. **ROUND TOP**

This mountain with the rounded summit that inspires its name stands taller than any other peak in the Carson Pass area, and boasts an outstanding payoff view. Round Top provides a step up in hiking distance, height, and overall difficulty from its neighbor Elephants Back, but still qualifies as a moderate day trip.

Distance: 8 miles round-trip (mostly on trails)
Time: 4 to 6 hours
Difficulty: Class 2; moderate to strenuous (for distance, elevation gain, and summit scramble)

Parking: Carson Pass lot
Trailhead elevation: 8,574 feet
Summit elevation: 10,381 feet
Elevation gain: 1,807 feet
Best season: June–Oct
Permits: None needed

FINDING THE TRAILHEAD

Park beside Highway 88 at Carson Pass, which charges a parking fee in summer and fall months, and requires a Sno-Park pass (not available on-site) Nov 1–May 30. GPS: N38 41.661' / W119 59.324'

CLIMBING THE MOUNTAIN

Hike south through the woods on the Pacific Crest Trail, passing Frog Lake. Turn right at the trail junction toward Winnemucca Lake, leaving the PCT and passing Elephants Back on your left. Winnemucca Lake provides a great opportunity for pictures of the mountain and a break before the steeper climbing starts.

Continue on the trail as you climb about 350 feet to Round Top Lake. Here a summit trail splits off to the left and climbs to the saddle between Round Top and The Sisters to its west. Switchbacks lead up the northwest slope, which may have snowfields early in the season. The rocky path takes you to the summit ridge, topped by dark volcanic basalt towers.

Most climbers stop and declare victory at the western tower, where the trail leads via Class 2 terrain. Those who must stand atop the true summit should continue to the east tower. This requires a traverse of the summit ridge and about 25 feet of Class 3 scrambling. Rock climbers may enjoy this, but the western tower is a better stopping point for children, dogs, and those uncomfortable with heights.

Either way, revel in the reward you've earned, which is a grand view of Deadwood Peak, The Sisters, Caples Lake, Red Lake Peak, and much more in Mokelumne and Carson–Iceberg Wildernesses.

> **SIERRA SECRETS**
>
> If the Carson Pass lot is full, you may find space in the Meiss trailhead lot, just to the west. For a longer hike, start at Woods Lake trailhead a few miles west of Carson Pass (for both options, the parking fee still applies).
>
> Winnemucca Lake at the base of the mountain apparently takes its name from a Paiute chief in Nevada. The name means "one moccasin."

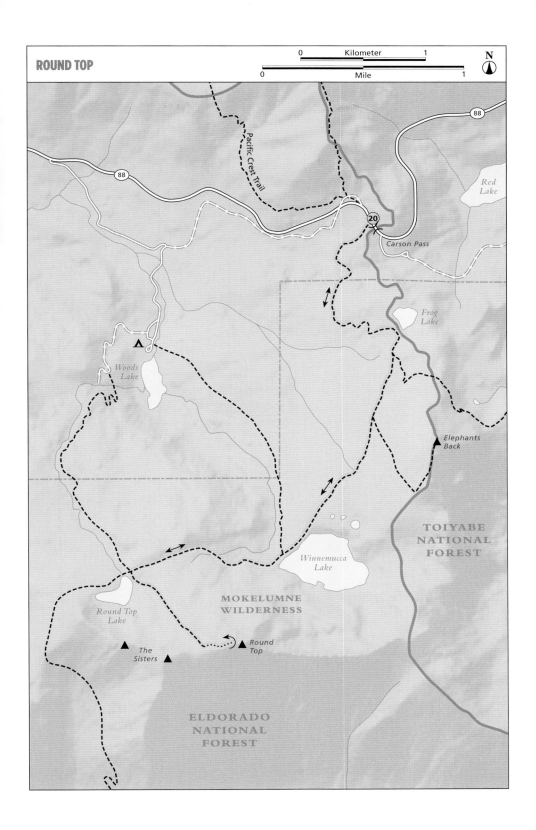

ROUND TOP

Pacific Crest Trail

88

Red Lake

20

Carson Pass

Frog Lake

Woods Lake

Elephants Back

TOIYABE NATIONAL FOREST

Winnemucca Lake

MOKELUMNE WILDERNESS

Round Top Lake

The Sisters

Round Top

ELDORADO NATIONAL FOREST

Caples Lake is visible from Round Top's summit.

HISTORY

Though settlers and miners once called the mountain "Silver Era Peak," members of the US Coast Survey bestowed its current name in 1877. In an effort to triangulate the mountain range, geographers made camp near the summit and exchanged heliotrope (reflected sunlight) signals with Mount Conness near Tioga Pass, starting in 1879, enduring difficult winter storms.

MILES AND DIRECTIONS

0.0   Start at Carson Pass and hike south on the PCT

1.2   At trail junction, stay right (south) on-trail to Winnemucca Lake

2.3   Stay left (west) at Winnemucca Lake and climb to Round Top Lake

3.3   Turn left (southeast) at Round Top Lake and ascend summit trail

4.0   Summit (western tower)

8.0   Arrive back at the trailhead

BONUS PEAKS IN THE CENTRAL SIERRA

MOUNT FINISKI

Elevation: 9,944 feet   **Difficulty:** Easy

Topping this fun peak takes just a short walk and a 500-foot climb, making a great outing for kids, beginners, or anyone who'd like a little high-elevation exercise. Park south of Highway 108 in a large pullout about a mile west of Sonora Pass. Mount Finiski (unnamed on many maps) stands just about 0.4 mile to the south. There is no established trail, so find a use trail or make your own line. Come in the spring to enjoy a snowy descent on skis, sleds, or snowboards. Accessible when the road opens in summer and fall, this outing takes about an hour. Conditions are best from July through October.

INSPIRATION POINT

Elevation: 7,940 feet   **Difficulty:** Easy

A breathtaking view awaits hikers who ascend this vista beside Lake Alpine on Highway 4. The trail climbs about 600 feet over the 1-mile trek to the top. Park near the Chickaree Picnic Area at the east side of the lake and find the trail leading southwest toward the shore. After about 0.3 mile, your route turns from the shoreline trail and leads south and uphill. Soon you will emerge from the trees as the path leads up the peak's western side. On the large summit plateau, you will find many interesting messages other visitors have written with rock letters. Expect to spend about two hours here. Conditions are best from May through November.

LEAVITT PEAK

Elevation: 11,573 feet   **Difficulty:** Strenuous

Climbers can achieve a true High Sierra peak within a day, but should prepare for a physical and challenging ascent. The mountain's name honors Hiram Leavitt, a Mono County judge who built an inn east of Sonora Pass in 1863. Park at Sonora Pass on Highway 108 and hike south on the Pacific Crest Trail. Starting at 9,643 feet, the path climbs rapidly over the next 5.5 miles, as wildflowers and waterfalls provide welcome diversions. Snow covers the trail on north-facing slopes in the early season; climbers may need crampons and ice axes to safely cross snowfields. After about 5 miles, find a use trail leading to the right (west), up the mountain's northeast slope, and then its eastern ridge. This 11-mile round-trip trek gains 1,930 feet and takes from six to ten hours. Some will enjoy this more as an overnight trip (permit required), and climbers should acclimate before attempting a summit this high. Conditions are best from July through September.

YOSEMITE NATIONAL PARK

Yosemite's towering rock walls, cascading waterfalls, rushing rivers, rounded domes, and tall mountains gush with grandeur like nowhere else. Seeing its splendor for the first time can touch one's soul, as reported Lafayette Bunnell, an author who entered the valley with the Mariposa Battalion in 1851.

"None but those who have visited this most wonderful valley can even imagine the feelings with which I looked upon the view that was there presented," he wrote. "As I looked, a peculiar exalted sensation seemed to fill my whole being, and I found my eyes in tears with emotion."

This majestic place has produced a similar response among Americans for well over a century, and from Native Americans for millennia. But its story dates back far longer than that.

GEOLOGY

As the climate began to cool about three million years ago, glaciers and icefields formed along the crest of the Sierra Nevada. Movement of these glaciers carved the granite peaks, walls, and domes that are visible in Yosemite today, just as rivers and streams before them cut canyons and valleys into the rock and carried vast amounts of sediment to the Central Valley.

Geologic processes continue in this glacier-carved marvel, even though the glaciers have largely disappeared. About eighty rockfalls occur per year, some of them dropping thousands of tons of granite from sheer formations like Half Dome, El Capitan, and Glacier Point. Streams deliver sediment into glacier-carved lake beds, slowly filling them until they become meadows, and plate movement continues to uplift the mountains at imperceptibly slow rates.

HISTORY

Native Americans lived in Yosemite Valley for some 8,000 years, according to archaeological evidence. But indigenous people believe they have been there since Ah-ha-le, Coyote-man, made the world and its people. The Ahwahneechee called their home *Ahwahnee*, meaning "place of the gaping mouth." One theory about the origin of the name *Yosemite* is that other tribes used it to refer to the Ahwahneechee, whom they feared, and that it means "they are killers." Seven contemporary tribes, including the Miwuk, trace their roots to Yosemite.

European Americans came into conflict with Native Americans after the Gold Rush brought prospectors to the foothills starting in 1849. Army major Jim Savage led fifty-seven men of the Mariposa Battalion into Yosemite Valley in 1851. The battalion burned down Ahwahneechee villages and forced their inhabitants to a reservation near Fresno. Some, like Chief Tenaya, later returned, but Indians' numbers in Yosemite dwindled as European Americans took control of the scenic jewel.

Yosemite Falls cascades down 2,425 feet from the north rim to the valley floor.

Tourism began in 1855 when James Hutchings and Thomas Ayers first visited and then publicized the area. Concerned about commercialization, US Senator John Conness and Galen Clark urged Congress and President Lincoln to authorize the Yosemite Grant Act in 1864. This protected Yosemite Valley and the Mariposa Grove of Giant Sequoias, setting the precedent for the future National Park Service. Stagecoach roads provided travelers with bumpy rides to the valley by the 1870s.

John Muir arrived in 1868, finding a job as a shepherd. While loggers downed giant sequoias and hacked through "tunnel trees" for photo opportunities and road tolls, Muir explored widely and penned articles about the Sierra Nevada. His writings helped to convince Congress to make Yosemite a national park in 1890. Muir's camping trip with President Teddy Roosevelt in 1903 led to greater federal protection of the initial Yosemite Grant, which had been under state control. Muir lost his final campaign to preserve Hetch Hetchy Valley when Congress authorized O'Shaughnessy Dam in 1913, but his legacy lives on in the wilderness he helped protect and the millions he inspired to the cause of conservation.

Chinese Americans played a unique role in the park's early years. The Gold Rush attracted them to California, but then the Legislature passed the prohibitive Foreign Miners Tax that forced them into other work. Some Chinese labored to build Yosemite's main roads in the 1870s and 1880s. Others worked in the Wawona Hotel. One who gained attention another way was Tie Sing. For twenty-one years, the affable cook amazed government cartographers doing backcountry research with culinary offerings fit for the Ahwahnee dining room, like fried chicken and hot apple pie. In gratitude they named 10,552-foot Sing Peak in honor of "the gourmet chef of the Sierra" in 1899.

Tioga Pass Road was completed in 1916. Soon paved roads led to private automobile traffic, travelers' facilities, and rapidly increasing visitation that continues to this day. This has allowed millions of people to experience Yosemite, and many have done remarkable and laudable things there. Ranger Enid Michael wrote 537 articles about the park, the most by any author. Artist Chiura Obata produced more than 100 watercolor paintings and woodblock prints of Yosemite and the Sierra Nevada following his visit in 1927, impressing audiences in both California and his native Japan. Miwok Chris Brown, also known as Chief Lemee, performed Native American dances for visitors for more than twenty years. Lucy Telles, descended of Paiute and Miwuk, made beautiful baskets in traditional style for twenty-five years. Photographer Ansel Adams captured breathtaking images for more than fifty years. Climbers like John Salathé, Royal Robbins, Warren Harding, Lynn Hill, Hans Florine, Steve Schneider, Tommy Caldwell, Beth Rodden, and Alex Honnold redefined the word "possible" while scaling steep and enormous granite walls, establishing Camp 4 as an international climbing mecca. Ranger Shelton Johnson served the park for more than a quarter-century, researching and teaching about the Buffalo Soldiers' service there, and winning a Superior Service Award from the Department of the Interior. Actor Lee Stetson portrayed John Muir in live performances for more than three decades. John Dill and Werner Braun each served more than forty years on the Yosemite Search and Rescue Team, which has saved thousands of people from distress and danger since 1974.

Yet the population boom has had drawbacks. More than five million people visited the park in 2016, a record. Traffic and lines diminish the visitor experience, but a greater problem is the threat people pose to the ecosystem. Hikers trample sensitive meadows. Dozens of drivers hit bears every year, and rangers have to euthanize others who become

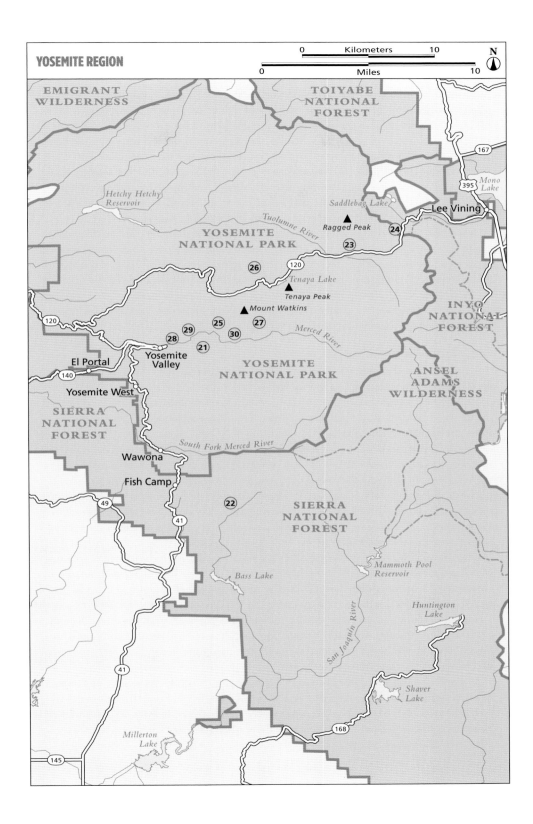

attracted to human food. Automobiles and campfires hurt air quality. Now more than ever, the National Park Service faces a daunting challenge in fulfilling its twin mandates to provide access to the public's land while also preserving it.

Thankfully, those who love the park work tirelessly to protect and share it. Yosemite Conservancy has spent hundreds of millions of dollars on conservation projects; notable achievements include the recovery of the peregrine falcon population and a great reduction in human–bear conflicts, thanks to visitor education and metal food lockers. A three-year, $40 million project to protect the Mariposa Grove concluded in 2018. NatureBridge provides educational experiences for thousands of students. Ranger Mauricio Escobar and José González, founder of Latino Outdoors, have introduced immigrants and Spanish speakers to the park. And noted climber Ron Kauk created Sacred Rok, a nonprofit group that brings underprivileged youth to Yosemite.

While the 1851 arrival of Bunnell and the Mariposa Battalion heralded terrible suffering to the Ahwahneechee and other tribes, Native Americans have endured and increased their presence in the park in recent years. James Johnson and Jay Johnson, both Miwuk and retired NPS employees, began an effort to restore an Indian village to the valley in 1977. That drive to preserve Native American historical and cultural heritage required decades of persistence, but neared completion in 2018. As tribal elder Bill Tucker said while visiting the construction site, "This is home."

VISITOR INFORMATION

Yosemite has an entrance fee (per car, per week). Alternatively, you can purchase an annual pass to all national parks and monuments.

Concerning camping, the park offers reservations six months in advance; valley sites for the peak summer season get snatched up in minutes, so plan ahead. Sites outside the valley are more attainable.

Visitors can obtain wilderness permits free of charge at the wilderness office in Yosemite Valley and at other locations. You can also reserve them up to six months in advance; a permit fee applies, plus an additional per-person fee for each member of the group. The park sets aside 60 percent of permits for reservations and 40 percent for walk-up visitors, starting at 11 a.m. daily for permits valid starting the following day. Popular trailheads like Happy Isles and Tuolumne Meadows book up early, so it's a good idea to make reservations if you plan to depart from them.

Tioga Road/Highway 120, which offers access to this collection's peaks near Tuolumne Meadows, closes to automobiles each winter with the first heavy snowfall, usually in November. Its opening date normally arrives in May, and sometimes June in a big snow year. Check the park website for road status.

Yosemite's visitation averages around four million per year, with the greatest numbers from June through September. Unfortunately, the park has become so popular that Yosemite Valley visitors in these months suffer through hours-long traffic jams in search of parking spaces, especially on weekends.

To avoid such aggravation, consider these suggestions. Visit in April, May, or October when conditions are quite nice and crowds are lighter. If you come in summer, arrive early and avoid the weekends, especially holiday weekends. Also, most people visit only Yosemite Valley, so you will avoid much of the fray by going to Tuolumne Meadows or other areas of interest instead.

21. SENTINEL DOME

Sentinel Dome claims the highest point on the south rim of Yosemite Valley, yet it's among the easiest peaks in Yosemite—and in this book—providing a perfect introductory "climb" for beginners and kids. The trailhead is right on the way for those driving to or from popular Glacier Point, so there's no excuse to miss it.

Distance: 2.4 miles round-trip (all on trails)	**Trailhead elevation:** 7,700 feet
Time: 1 hour	**Summit elevation:** 8,122 feet
Difficulty: Class 1; easy	**Elevation gain:** 422 feet
Parking: Sentinel Dome/Taft Point trailhead lot	**Best season:** June–Nov
	Permits: None needed

FINDING THE TRAILHEAD

 Drivers will find Sentinel Dome/Taft Point trailhead parking lot on the northwest side of Glacier Point Road, about 0.75 mile southwest from Glacier Point's parking lot. GPS: N37 42.742' / W119 35.176'

CLIMBING THE MOUNTAIN

A signed trail leads northeast through jeffrey and ponderosa pines; in season, you may also enjoy phlox, larkspur, and penstemon wildflowers.

Soon the dome will come into view. Follow the trail to its northeast before climbing its gentlest flank to the rounded summit. From here you can see much of Yosemite Valley and the park's northern high country. Right beneath you is Sentinel Rock and straight

---

SIERRA SECRETS

Hikers can reach nearby Taft Point from the same trailhead. The name of this overlook honors President William Taft (1857–1930). Like his predecessor Teddy Roosevelt before him, the twenty-seventh president also visited Yosemite in the company of John Muir, in 1909, and had lunch near the landmark that now carries his name. Taft Point stands atop a tall and sheer cliff; visitors can look down through its fissures (cracks in its granite) and see Yosemite Valley thousands of feet below. Taft Point also features a unique and impressive view of El Capitan. The round-trip hike is 2 miles long on Pohono Trail.

Sentinel Dome makes an excellent winter peak for those skiing or snowshoeing from Yosemite Ski and Snowboard Area (formerly called Badger Pass) to Glacier Point. This 21-mile round-trip trek normally takes two days and involves an overnight camp (permit required), or a stay at Glacier Point Ski Hut. The preferred winter route differs from the summer trail. Traveling east on Glacier Point Road, pass the Sentinel Dome/Taft Point trailhead. When the road turns sharply right in about 0.7 mile, go straight (west) instead to climb to a saddle south of the dome. Climb counterclockwise to the north to the summit.

Sentinel Dome

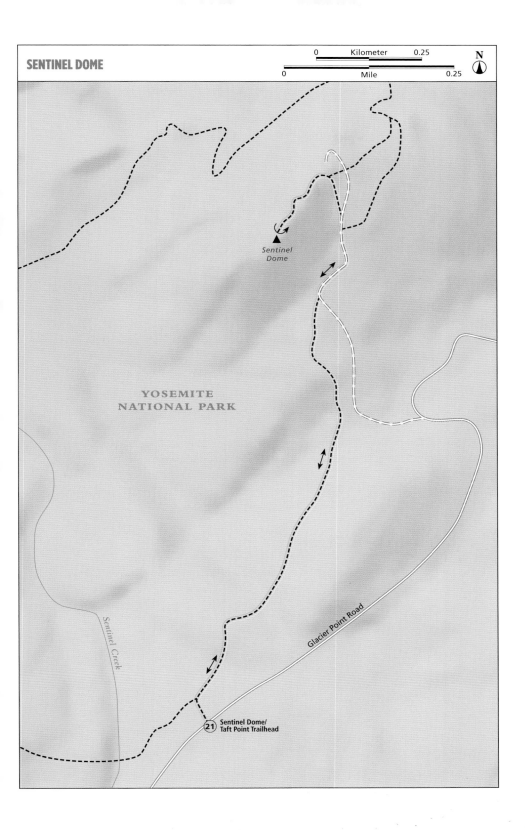

0   Kilometer   0.25

0   Mile   0.25

N

YOSEMITE
NATIONAL PARK

Sentinel
Dome

Sentinel Creek

Glacier Point Road

21 Sentinel Dome/
Taft Point Trailhead

Scouts, including the author's father, Tom Johanson, visit Sentinel Dome's famous jeffrey pine in 1952.

ahead is Yosemite Falls. Be sure to also pay your respects to the fallen jeffrey pine that stood for centuries.

HISTORY

Atop Sentinel Dome lived a picturesque jeffrey pine for an estimated 400 years. Incredibly, the tree grew out of granite with no visible soil on a high, windswept perch. Thousands of photographers, including Ansel Adams, captured its image as early as 1867. Though admirers brought it buckets of water in a severe drought, the tree died in 1977, standing twenty-six more years before falling down in 2003.

MILES AND DIRECTIONS

0.0   Start at Sentinel Dome/Taft Point trailhead and hike northwest

0.1   Turn right (northeast) at trail junction

1.2   Summit

2.4   Arrive back at the trailhead

22. FRESNO DOME

This destination just a few miles from Yosemite's southern border reaps several benefits from its location outside the park, such as no entrance fee and few visitors. But you'll still get an easy and pleasant climb onto a granite peak that looks more difficult than it is, with a beautiful and little-known grove of giant sequoias on the way as an added bonus.

Distance: 1.6 miles round-trip (all on trails)
Time: 1 hour
Difficulty: Class 1; easy
Parking: Dirt lot beside Sierra National FR 6S10

Trailhead elevation: 7,300 feet
Summit elevation: 7,540 feet
Elevation gain: 240 feet
Best season: June–Oct
Permits: None needed

FINDING THE TRAILHEAD

From the junction of Highways 49 and 41 in Oakhurst, drive north on Highway 41 for 4 miles and look for a Sierra Sky Ranch sign on the east side of the road. Turn right (east) onto FR 632 (signed as Sky Ranch Road) and follow the signs for Fresno Dome Campground. Take the road as it meanders northeast and becomes FR 6S10. After you reach the campground at 13.3 miles, continue on 6S10—as it becomes curvy, steep, and rougher—for another 2.8 miles, to a signed trailhead and parking area. GPS: N37 27.611' / W119 31.727'

SIERRA SECRETS

Fresno is Spanish for "ash trees," which line San Joaquin River. While no documentation explaining the mountain's renaming has been found, the dome and much of the river were once part of Fresno County, which could explain the change.

No trip to this area is complete without a visit to the Nelder Grove of Giant Sequoias. Look for a turnoff 6.3 miles from the Highway 41 turnoff. Shadow of the Giants Trail visits twelve sequoias in just a 1-mile loop. This was once called Fresno Grove, but now carries the name of John Nelder, a 49er who gave up on mining gold, built a cabin here in 1875, and lived in it until his death in 1889.

CLIMBING THE MOUNTAIN

This mountain stands in Sierra National Forest a few miles south of Yosemite's southern entrance as the eagle flies. This is why most Yosemite visitors have never been here, so take the path less traveled for a change.

A trail from the parking lot leads southwest through thick trees that soon give way to a meadow. Then the north slope of the granite dome comes into view and the trail climbs up its rocky slope to the summit. Tree-covered hills of Sierra National Forest fill our view.

Fresno Dome

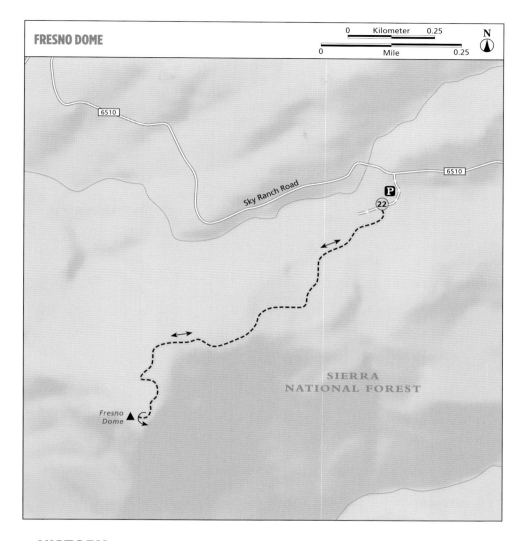

SIERRA
NATIONAL FOREST

Fresno
Dome

HISTORY

Mono called this granite peak *Wamello*, meaning "the greeting place." Both John Muir and the Whitney Survey published that name in the 1870s, but the current name appeared on maps starting in 1912, and anyone who knows the reason for the change isn't talking.

MILES AND DIRECTIONS

0.0   Hike southwest from the parking area

0.5   Ascend dome's gentle northern slope

0.8   Summit

1.6   Arrive back at the trailhead

23. LEMBERT DOME

Lembert Dome looks like a big mountain and feels like one from its summit, but requires just a fairly short and gentle trek to stand atop it. Hiking across its slanted granite near the top may feel awkward, but the ascent requires no climbing expertise. Every day in summer and fall, many hikers reach its novel perch and enjoy its inspiring view of Tuolumne Meadows.

Distance: 2.2 miles round-trip (on trails and over granite)
Time: 2 to 3 hours
Difficulty: Class 1; easy to moderate
Parking: Dog Lake trailhead lot

Trailhead elevation: 8,950 feet
Lembert Dome elevation: 9,450 feet
Elevation gain: 500 feet
Best season: June–Oct
Permits: None needed

FINDING THE TRAILHEAD

From Highway 120, turn south onto Tuolumne Meadows Lodge Road, drive past the ranger station on your left, and park in the Dog Lake trailhead lot. GPS: N37 52.705' / W119 20.341'

CLIMBING THE MOUNTAIN

Hike north, cross Highway 120, and join the trail that climbs switchbacks up Lembert's southeastern slope.

You'll quickly climb above the lodgepoles to the shoulder of the mountain's eastern side. Leave the dirt trail to climb a westbound use path up the granite slope. The summit initially in sight is a false one, but the glorious views of Tuolumne Meadows are real, and get better with every step as you traverse the mountain's rocky spine.

Soon a rounded knob, which is the real summit, comes into view. The eastern side facing you is steep enough to challenge rock climbers, but hikers have a more moderate alternative. Continue hiking west across the sloped granite toward its south (left) side. Circle clockwise around the knob, passing its southern face, and ascend the gentler west face instead. Cathedral Peak, Mount Conness, Ragged Peak, Mount Lyell, and Tuolumne River are a few highlights of your panoramic view.

If you're looking for variety and a longer hike, you can complete a loop around Lembert Dome and visit Dog Lake just north of the mountain. From the summit, simply retrace your steps across the granite back to the dirt path on the mountain's eastern shoulder. Then turn left instead of right, making a counterclockwise circle. A spur trail from the top of the loop leads to Dog Lake, another optional detour. The loop leads to Lembert Dome's parking area. From here, cross Tioga Road and take the eastbound trail back to the Dog Lake trailhead parking lot. The loop and summit make a 4-mile trip, or 5 miles if you also visit Dog Lake.

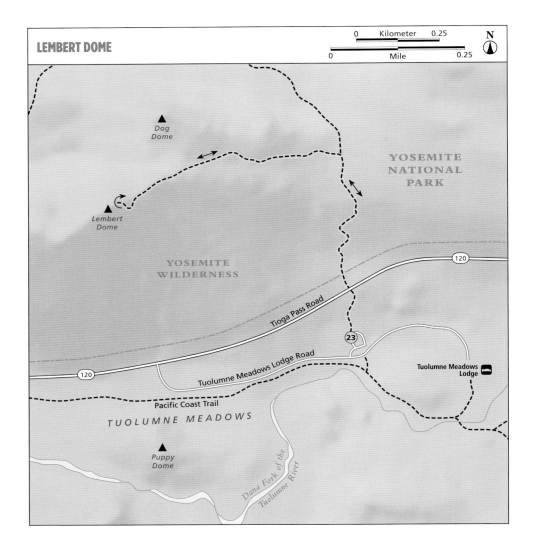

0   Kilometer   0.25

0   Mile   0.25

N

YOSEMITE
NATIONAL
PARK

Dog
Dome

Lembert
Dome

YOSEMITE
WILDERNESS

Tioga Pass Road

120

23

Tuolumne Meadows
Lodge

120

Tuolumne Meadows Lodge Road

Pacific Coast Trail

TUOLUMNE MEADOWS

Puppy
Dome

Dana Fork of the
Tuolumne River

SIERRA SECRETS

Geologists believe ice completely overtopped the dome during the last major glaciation. A glacier flowed up and polished the dome's smooth and gentle side. Ice picked up large blocks of rock from the steeper side and carried them away.

For winter enthusiasts passing this way on skis or snowshoes, Lembert Dome offers a fine day trip from Tuolumne Ski Hut (which serves as the Tuolumne Meadows Campground office in summer). Approaching from either Yosemite Valley or Lee Vining will likely require a few days in each direction, but it's well worth it, as Tuolumne Meadows in winter provides an unforgettable experience.

A hiker approaches the summit of Lembert Dome.

HISTORY

This mountain gets its name from hermit John Lembert, the first white settler in Tuolumne Meadows. Lembert claimed 160 acres there in 1885, built a log cabin in which he lived, constructed another shelter that still stands in ruins over nearby Soda Springs, and raised goats until he lost them in the winter storms of 1889–1890. Lembert continued to summer in Tuolumne Meadows, but spent the colder months in a cabin near El Portal, where he was murdered in the winter of 1896–1897 in an apparent robbery.

MILES AND DIRECTIONS

0.0   Start at Dog Lake trailhead and hike north

0.1   Cross Highway 120 and continue north

0.5   Go left (west) at summit trail junction

1.1   Summit

2.2   Arrive back at the trailhead

24. **GAYLOR PEAK**

Starting from a high pass, hiking only a mile, and gaining just over 1,000 feet, this might be the easiest 11,000 footer that you ever climb on the right day. Add a scenic view and an interesting history, and Gaylor Peak has all the elements of a short but enjoyable adventure.

Distance: 2 miles round-trip (on trails and use trails)
Time: 1 to 2 hours
Difficulty: Class 1; moderate (for elevation)
Parking: Tioga Pass entrance station lot

Trailhead elevation: 9,943 feet
Summit elevation: 11,004 feet
Elevation gain: 1,061 feet
Best season: July–Oct
Permits: None needed

FINDING THE TRAILHEAD

 Park in the lot on the north side of Highway 120 just west of the Tioga Pass entrance station. If the lot is full, you can also park beside the highway just east of the entrance station. GPS: N37 54.613' / W119 15.497'

CLIMBING THE MOUNTAIN

Take the signed trail toward Gaylor Lakes and start your brisk climb through scattered and hardy whitebark and lodgepole pines.

Hikers will reach a pass between Gaylor Peak and the Gaylor Lakes after 0.5 mile. Turn off the well-traveled trail to the lake and instead follow a use trail toward the right. You'll reach the summit after another 0.5 mile.

From here you'll see features such as Middle Gaylor Lake, Granite Lakes, Lee Vining Canyon, Mount Dana, the Cathedral Range, and much more.

If you're ready for a little more adventure before returning, the trail to Middle Gaylor Lake, around it, and back to the saddle adds just 1.3 miles to your outing. That's where to go for the best pictures of Gaylor Peak.

HISTORY

During the mining days of the Tioga Pass area, prospectors knew the peak as "Tioga Hill." But now it carries the name of Andrew Jack Gaylor (1846–1921), one of the first Yosemite rangers during his last fourteen years of life. Gaylor had also served as a civilian packmaster during the Spanish-American War. Before shipping out with the Rough Riders, he wrote these words of advice to his son: "Love many, trust few, and always paddle your own canoe."

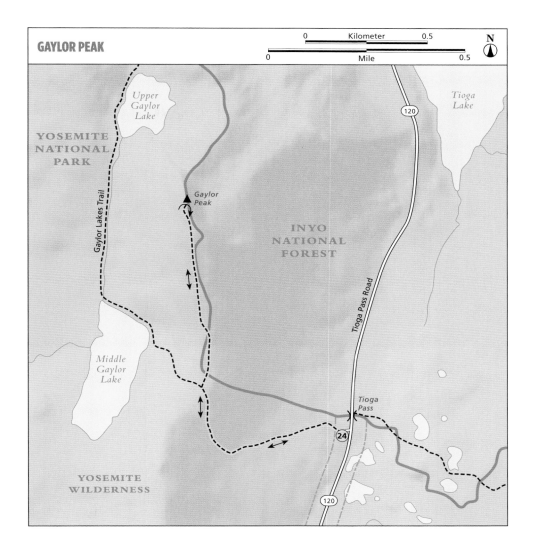

SIERRA SECRETS

Though this outing is short in both distance and elevation gain, the high elevation of the starting point and summit make this a better choice for those who have spent a few days in the mountains than for those who just drove up from sea level.

Gaylor Peak makes a nice snowy adventure for cross-country skiers and snowshoers soon after Tioga Road opens to automobiles in May or June.

Anglers report good fishing at Gaylor and Granite Lakes.

MILES AND DIRECTIONS

0.0   From Tioga Pass parking area, hike west on Gaylor Lakes Trail

0.5   At the pass, leave Gaylor Lakes Trail and turn right (north) onto a use trail

1.0   Summit

2.0   Arrive back at the trailhead

25. **NORTH DOME**

Here's a rare mountain with a summit lower than its trailhead, but climbers will still feel on top of the world as they look down on Yosemite Valley. The moderate hike includes some gentle ups and downs and an optional detour to the interesting Indian Rock formation. North Dome's summit boasts the best views of Half Dome and Clouds Rest in the park.

Distance: 9.6 miles round-trip (all on trails)	**Trailhead elevation:** 8,150 feet
Time: 4 to 6 hours	**Summit elevation:** 7,542 feet
Difficulty: Class 1; moderate (for distance)	**Elevation gain:** -608 feet
Parking: Porcupine Creek trailhead lot	**Best season:** June–Nov
	Permits: None needed

FINDING THE TRAILHEAD

Park beside Highway 120 at Porcupine Creek trailhead; don't confuse this with Porcupine Flat Campground a mile to the west. GPS: N37 48.393' / W119 32.712'

CLIMBING THE MOUNTAIN

Our trail to the south leads over an old paved road for the first 0.7 mile, through fern-filled meadows and across Porcupine Creek. This is the last reliable source of water until you return here. You will pass a few trail junctions in the first 2 miles. Simply follow the signs for North Dome through the forest of jeffrey pines and lodgepole pines. At about 2.8 miles, a trail sign and junction appear for Indian Rock, a natural arch formation atop a hill 0.3 mile to the northeast. This is a worthy detour, but afternoon light makes it more photogenic, so you may want to check it out on your return trip.

Continuing south, the forest thins and gives way to granite slabs. Be alert here: The trail is harder to follow than the path through the trees, although it's fairly clear as long as it's free of snow.

Soon North Dome itself comes into view, and our trail leads us down into a small gully beside it before climbing the final steps to its summit. From here you can look over much of Yosemite Valley and Tenaya Canyon, and Half Dome appears close enough to touch.

HISTORY

Ahwahneechee believed their Great Spirit had punished a husband and wife for "wickedness" and turned them both into stone. According to legends, the man Nangas became the mountain now called North Dome, the woman Tis-si-ak became Half Dome, and the basket she threw at her husband in anger became nearby Basket Dome.

North Dome

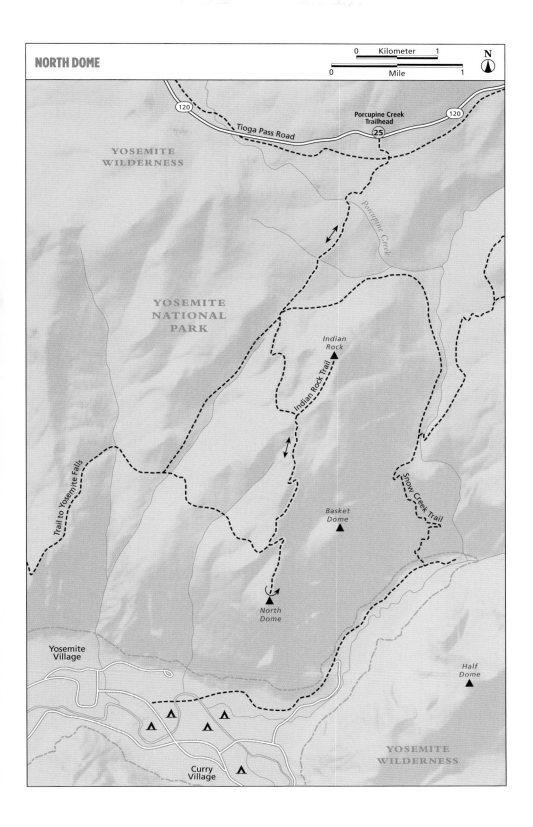

NORTH DOME

N

0   Kilometer   1

0   Mile   1

120

Tioga Pass Road

Porcupine Creek
Trailhead

120

25

YOSEMITE
WILDERNESS

Porcupine Creek

YOSEMITE
NATIONAL
PARK

Indian
Rock

Indian Rock Trail

Snow Creek Trail

Trail to Yosemite Falls

Basket
Dome

North
Dome

Yosemite
Village

Half
Dome

Curry
Village

YOSEMITE
WILDERNESS

Visiting Indian Rock involves just a short detour.

MILES AND DIRECTIONS

0.0   Hike southwest from Porcupine Creek trailhead

1.7   Stay right (south) at Snow Creek trail junction

1.8   Turn left (south) at Yosemite Falls trail junction

2.8   Stay right (south) at Indian Rock trail junction

4.8   Summit

9.6   Arrive back at the trailhead

SIERRA SECRETS

Some think Chief Tenaya's face appears on the southwest face of Clouds Rest. North Dome's summit is the best place to see this. Light and shadow make it most visible on clear days from mid-morning to noon.

Sunlight illuminates the sheer face of Half Dome from mid-afternoon to early evening on clear days.

26. MOUNT HOFFMANN

Considering effort and payoff, Mount Hoffmann might be the best summit experience in Yosemite. A moderate climb leads to a commanding view of virtually every major peak in the park. As an added bonus, hikers will pass beautiful May Lake on the way up and back down again. Don't underestimate the altitude, though; this is an outing for fit climbers who have acclimated to the elevation.

Distance: 6.2 miles round-trip (on trails and use trails)
Time: 3 to 5 hours
Difficulty: Class 2; moderate to strenuous (for distance, elevation, and elevation gain)

Parking: May Lake trailhead lot
Trailhead elevation: 8,860 feet
Summit elevation: 10,850 feet
Elevation gain: 1,990 feet
Best season: June–Oct
Permits: None needed

FINDING THE TRAILHEAD

 From Highway 120, take the May Lake turnoff about 2.2 miles east of Olmsted Point. Drive north on the rough but paved road 1.7 miles to a parking area. GPS: N37 49.958' / W119 29.460'

CLIMBING THE MOUNTAIN

Take the trail leading north for about a mile and gaining 500 feet to May Lake, at 9,329 feet of elevation.

From the lake's southeast corner, a right turn would take you to May Lake High Sierra Camp. But our path lies left as you hike west along the lake's southern shore. Pretty as the lake is, park rules do not allow swimming here, and the water would be uncomfortably cold anyway. Hop over Snow Creek on your way to the southwest corner, where you may want to refill your water bottle. From here the route turns southwest and the climb resumes.

The trail to the summit is unofficial and unmaintained, but rock cairns and footprints make it clear enough after snow melts in the early summer. From the lake, our climb quickly ascends above the tree line and gains about 1,500 feet in the last mile, which is one good reason to take your time. More than 100 different kinds of wildflowers growing here provide another reason to take it slow and

---

SIERRA SECRETS

Bring a map, whether or not you use it for the climb, to help identify the dozens of peaks visible from the summit.

Most climbers will pass right by May Lake High Sierra Camp, which offers food and lodging in summer to those with reservations.

If you want to make a call around here, there's generally a cell-phone service box at the Highway 120 turnoff to May Lake.

Very ambitious cross-country skiers and snowshoers make this a winter destination.

Mount Hoffmann

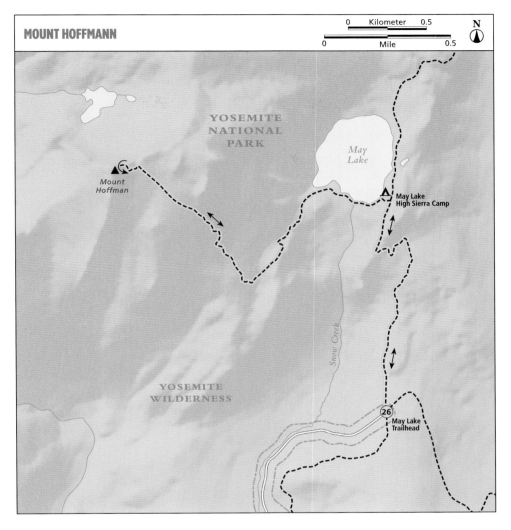

Kilometer

Mile

N

YOSEMITE
NATIONAL
PARK

May
Lake

Mount
Hoffman

May Lake
High Sierra Camp

Snow Creek

YOSEMITE
WILDERNESS

26 May Lake
Trailhead

easy. The final segment requires some Class 2 scrambling up granite slabs. Aim for the antenna that marks the summit.

From the top you'll see countless mountains in all directions. Particularly attractive are the views of nearby Hoffmann's Thumb, Half Dome, Clouds Rest, and the Clark Range. This is a great place to eat lunch, but watch out for the hungry marmots!

HISTORY

Members of the Whitney Survey made the first recorded ascent on June 24, 1863. William Brewer wrote that the summit "commanded a sublime view." The group named the mountain for Charles Hoffmann (1838–1913), the survey's principal topographer. John Muir followed in their footsteps six years later, and was so impressed that he encouraged those wishing to experience the best of Yosemite to "go straight to Mount Hoffmann. From the summit nearly all of the Yosemite Park is displayed like a map."

May Lake borders the summit trail.

MILES AND DIRECTIONS

0.0   Hike north from May Lake trailhead

1.0   Turn left (west) at May Lake and hike west on a use trail

3.1   Summit

6.2   Arrive back at the trailhead

27. **CLOUDS REST**

Clouds Rest gets just a fraction of the traffic Half Dome sees daily in summer months, yet it's a better experience in several ways. Taller than its more famous neighbor by more than 1,000 feet, Clouds Rest also offers a shorter hike, less climbing, and an incredible summit view that's among the best in the Sierra Nevada.

Distance: 14.2 miles round-trip (all on trails)
Time: 6 to 8 hours
Difficulty: Class 2; moderate to strenuous (for distance and elevation gain)

Parking: Sunrise Lakes trailhead lot
Trailhead elevation: 8,150 feet
Summit elevation: 9,926 feet
Elevation gain: 1,776 feet
Best season: June–Sept
Permits: None needed

FINDING THE TRAILHEAD

Take Highway 120 to the west side of Tenaya Lake and park beside the road or in the Sunrise Lakes trailhead lot. GPS: N37 49.545' / W119 28.206'

CLIMBING THE MOUNTAIN

Hike east and quickly cross the lake's southwest outlet, which may require wading early in the season. Follow the trail as it turns south and climbs switchbacks up a steep ridge. After you gain around 1,000 feet, the hardest part of this outing will be behind you.

Next our trail levels off and reaches a fork. The three picturesque Sunrise Lakes are within a mile to the left, providing great swimming on a hot summer day. But for Clouds Rest, stay right on the trail, which leads south through pine trees. A small pond about a mile from the junction is your best bet for water late in the season. At the next trail junction, stay right on Clouds Rest Trail, leading southwest.

Finally you will face the rocky climb up a narrow ridge to the summit, the psychological crux of the route. Deep drops to the sides have intimidated many, but the hike itself is simple and manageable.

Enjoy your summit view, which includes dozens of prominent Yosemite peaks. Among them are North Dome, Basket Dome, Mount Watkins, Mount Conness, Matthes Crest, Mount Starr King, and, of course, Half Dome.

HISTORY

Members of the Mariposa Battalion named the mountain in 1851 when they saw clouds settling on the peak before snow. That ominous sign sent them scurrying back to camp to weather the storm. Tenaya Canyon runs southwest of the peak, and according to folklore, carries the Ahwahneechee chief's curse, which he angrily pronounced after battalion soldiers killed his youngest son. In the right light, some even see Tenaya's wrathful face on the side of the mountain.

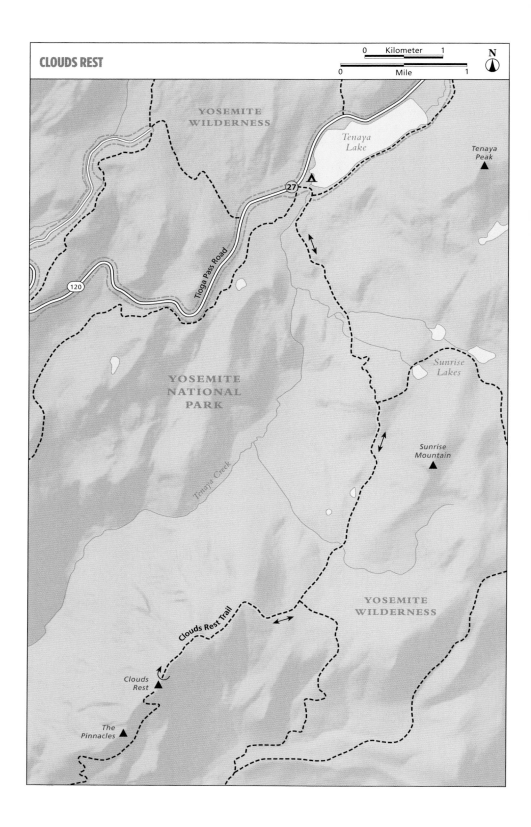

N

0 Kilometer 1

0 Mile 1

YOSEMITE
WILDERNESS

*Tenaya
Lake*

*Tenaya
Peak*

27

Tioga Pass Road

120

YOSEMITE
NATIONAL
PARK

*Sunrise
Lakes*

Tenaya Creek

*Sunrise
Mountain*

Clouds Rest Trail

YOSEMITE
WILDERNESS

*Clouds
Rest*

*The
Pinnacles*

Clouds Rest and Half Dome overlook Tenaya Canyon.

MILES AND DIRECTIONS

0.0   Hike east from Sunrise Lakes trailhead

0.2   Turn right (south) at a trail junction and hike uphill

2.5   Stay right (south) at a trail junction

4.7   Stay right (southwest) at a trail junction

7.1   Summit

14.2   Arrive back at the trailhead

SIERRA SECRETS

Chief Tenaya's face on the southwest face is best viewed on sunny days from North Dome from mid-morning until around noon.

Snow can cover the trail early in the season, especially after a big winter, greatly increasing the difficulty of route finding. If that's the case, come back later. Carry a map and compass in any event.

Several variations may appeal to overnight backpackers. The trail leading to Yosemite Valley (4.7 miles from the start) and a trail leading south from the summit both connect to the John Muir Trail. The JMT leads northeast past Sunrise High Sierra Camp and Cathedral Lakes to Tuolumne Meadows, or southwest past the Half Dome Trail, Nevada Fall, and Vernal Fall to Happy Isles. Permits are required for overnight travel.

28. **EL CAPITAN**

Rock climbers worldwide labor for years to achieve the summit of El Capitan, but fit hikers can reach it and return in a day. Compared to its rival Half Dome, El Cap offers an easier hike, fewer permitting challenges, and just as grand a view.

Distance: 16 miles (all on trails)
Time: 8 to 12 hours
Difficulty: Class 1; moderate to strenuous (for distance)
Parking: Tamarack Flat

Trailhead elevation: 6,300 feet
Summit elevation: 7,735 feet
Elevation gain: 1,435 feet
Best season: June and July
Permits: None needed

FINDING THE TRAILHEAD

Starting from Crane Flat, take Highway 120 east for 3.8 miles. Then turn right on Old Big Oak Flat Road, drive to Tamarack Flat Campground, and park. GPS: N37 45.138' / W119 44.226'

CLIMBING THE MOUNTAIN

Start your hike on Old Big Oak Flat Road, heading east through a lodgepole pine forest. Paved at first, the route steadily descends as you approach and cross a bridge over Cascade Creek. Then watch out for your left turn, where the trail parts from the road descending into Yosemite Valley.

Next begins a climb through white firs and sugar pines to steep slopes covered with manzanita. Meadows full of wildflowers waiting above will reward your toil. Take a break at Ribbon Creek, possibly the last source of water until the summit.

Take the spur trail to explore the rounded summit of El Capitan. Enjoy the view of Yosemite Valley, especially the Cathedral Rocks and Cathedral Spires to the south, which look close enough to touch.

SIERRA SECRETS

Consider timing carefully for this trip. Drivers bound for Tamarack Flat must wait for the Tioga Pass opening, usually in late spring. But the streams that supply water on the route dry up by late summer. June and July are ideal. When Ribbon Falls (west of El Capitan) is visible from Yosemite Valley, you'll know that Ribbon Creek is still flowing.

To make this trip in spring before Tioga Pass opens, start from Old Big Oak Flat Trailhead on Big Oak Flat Road. This adds about 1.5 miles of hiking in each direction and about 1,500 feet of elevation gain, but makes the route accessible in cooler months, with more abundant water sources.

Some hikers enjoy this more as an overnight trip. If you intend to camp, obtain a wilderness permit. The Ribbon Creek area is your best bet for a good site near water.

El Capitan

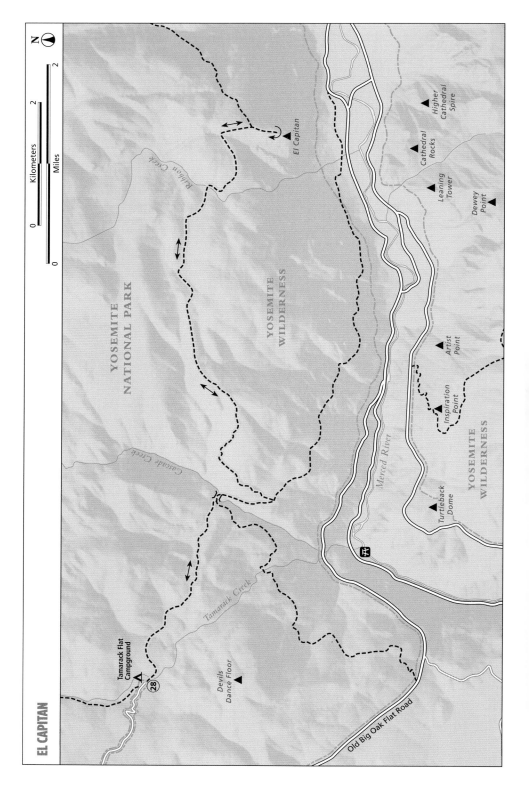

EL CAPITAN

N

Kilometers
0   2

Miles
0   2

YOSEMITE
NATIONAL PARK

YOSEMITE
WILDERNESS

YOSEMITE
WILDERNESS

Ribbon Creek

Cascade Creek

Tamarack Creek

Merced River

Tamarack Flat
Campground

28

Devils
Dance Floor

Old Big Oak Flat Road

El Capitan

Higher
Cathedral
Spire

Cathedral
Rocks

Leaning
Tower

Dewey
Point

Artist
Point

Inspiration
Point

Turtleback
Dome

HISTORY

The Miwuk called the mountain *Tu-Tok-A-Nu'-La*, based on the legend of a worm that climbed its steep face to save two bear cubs stranded atop it. Native Americans apparently had various names for the granite monolith, with multiple meanings. Some knew it as "Crane Mountain" in honor of the sand cranes that flew over it, and others called it "Giant's Tower." Members of the Mariposa Battalion named it El Capitan in 1851.

MILES AND DIRECTIONS

0.0   Start from Tamarack Flat and hike east

1.9   Stay left (east) at trail junction

2.1   Cross the bridge over Cascade Creek

2.6   Turn left (northwest) at trail junction

6.3   Cross Ribbon Creek and continue hiking

7.6   Turn right (south) at junction onto spur trail to summit

8.0   Summit

16.0 Arrive back at the trailhead

Visiting El Capitan's rounded top makes a fine one-day or overnight hike.

29. EAGLE PEAK

This proud perch above Yosemite Valley delivers compelling views of formations, including Half Dome and Sentinel Rock. Trails approach Eagle Peak from Yosemite Valley, El Capitan, and Highway 120, making many trip variations possible, yet it gets much less visitation than the park's other iconic destinations.

Distance: 12 miles round-trip (all on trails)
Time: 8 to 10 hours
Difficulty: Class 2; strenuous (for distance and elevation gain)
Parking: Yosemite Valley lots

Trailhead elevation: 4,000 feet
Summit elevation: 7,783 feet
Elevation gain: 3,783 feet
Best season: May–Oct
Permits: None needed

FINDING THE TRAILHEAD

Park in any Yosemite Valley public lot and walk or take a free shuttle bus to Camp 4 on Northside Drive. The Camp 4 lot is restricted to registered campers only, but there's a public lot across the road and southwest of the lodge. GPS: N37 44.543' / W119 36.126'

CLIMBING THE MOUNTAIN

Starting at Camp 4, the historic climbers' mecca, suits this adventure because we're going climbing. Take the signed Upper Yosemite Fall Trail. Dozens of switchbacks gain about 1,000 feet by Columbia Rock, a good spot to rest and enjoy the view. Now the route flattens for about a mile, still with some ups and downs. Then you get your first look at Upper Yosemite Fall. Soon after that, a spur splits from the main trail to an outlook with the trip's best view of the entire 2,425-foot waterfall. The route's next landmark is the winter closure gate. Most reach this in about half the time they take to reach the rim.

Switchbacks and gravel require careful footing. There's no shade on the upper portion of the trail, gaining 1,600 feet. A cool mist will ease your ascent early in the season, but expect a heat wave after the waterfall dries up in late summer.

Once you reach the rim, the trail splits; the path to the right leads to the Yosemite Falls viewing area, a worthy detour. Nearly all of your fellow hikers to this point are headed there. Our path lies to the left, though. Hike 0.5 mile to another junction where you turn left again (at the sign for Eagle Peak), and then another 2 miles, to our

SIERRA SECRETS

During summer and fall, consider hiking from Yosemite Creek Trailhead on Highway 120. Though a longer trek, at 15.6 miles round-trip, it requires much less climbing (just about 500 feet) and a less-tiring overall effort. Starting at Yosemite Creek or Tamarack Flat and finishing at Camp 4 are other possibilities, if you can arrange transportation. Though these options make long day trips, they are all enjoyable overnight outings for backpackers camping near the valley rim (wilderness permits required).

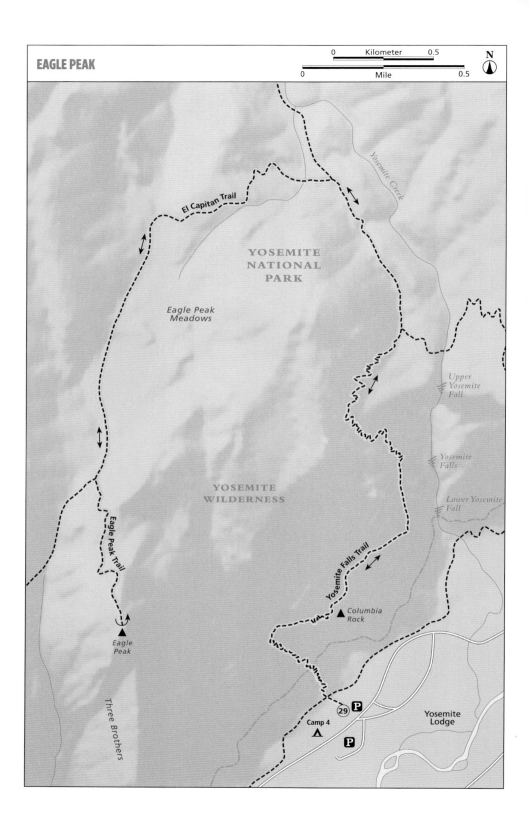

EAGLE PEAK

Kilometer
0   0.5

Mile
0   0.5

N

Yosemite Creek

El Capitan Trail

YOSEMITE
NATIONAL
PARK

*Eagle Peak
Meadows*

*Upper
Yosemite
Fall*

*Yosemite
Falls*

YOSEMITE
WILDERNESS

*Lower Yosemite
Fall*

Eagle Peak Trail

Yosemite Falls Trail

▲ *Columbia
Rock*

▲
*Eagle
Peak*

Three Brothers

29 P

Camp 4
⛺

P

*Yosemite
Lodge*

Eagle Peak's view features
Mount Starr King and the
Clark Range.

final split. Here the trail sign declares Eagle Peak 0.3 mile away. The actual distance is closer to a 0.5 mile, but it's worth it! Turn left for the final approach to the grand perch of eagles and mountain climbers, and the highest point of the valley's north rim.

HISTORY

Ahwahneechee called the triple-peak formation *Waw-haw-kee*, meaning "Falling Rocks." Members of the Mariposa Battalion renamed them Three Brothers in 1851. Eagle Peak, tallest of the siblings, was a favorite perch of its namesake bird of prey. "I once saw seven eagles here at play; they would skim out upon the air, one following the other, and then swoop perpendicularly down for a thousand or more feet, and then sail out again horizontally upon the air with such graceful nonchalance that one almost envied them their apparent gratification," wrote James Hutchings, who led a tourist group into Yosemite Valley in 1855.

MILES AND DIRECTIONS

0.0   From Camp 4, hike north on the signed Yosemite Falls Trail

1.0   Keep climbing past Columbia Rock to the north

3.0   Turn left (west) at Yosemite Falls trail junction

3.5   Turn left (west) at El Capitan trail junction

5.5   Turn left (south) at Eagle Peak trail junction

6.0   Summit

12.0 Arrive back at the trailhead

30. HALF DOME

Summiting the most picturesque mountain in Yosemite is a lifetime outdoors highlight for many. Ascending its steel cables requires a strong grip, cool nerves, and a high level of fitness, so prepare accordingly. The park limits the number of hikers, and requires permits to relieve overcrowding, so climbers need to plan ahead.

Distance: 16.4 miles round-trip (all on trails)
Time: 8 to 12 hours
Difficulty: Class 3; strenuous (for distance and elevation gain)
Parking: Public lots in Yosemite Valley

Trailhead elevation: 4,000 feet
Summit elevation: 8,839 feet
Elevation gain: 4,839 feet
Best season: June–Oct
Permits: Required

FINDING THE TRAILHEAD

Park in any of the valley's public lots and walk or take the free shuttle to Happy Isles trailhead at the east end of the valley. GPS: N37 43.967' / W119 33.469'

GETTING THE PERMIT

Yosemite has required permits and limited the number of hikers on Half Dome since 2011. While these regulations force climbers to plan ahead and wait their turn, they have reduced traffic on the cables, which was both unpleasant and dangerous. The following details were current upon publication of this guide, but Yosemite's permitting procedures are subject to change. Check nps.gov for the latest information.

The park allots 300 permits per day during the summer season while the cables are up, normally mid–May to mid–October, with 225 for day hikers and 75 for overnight backpackers.

Day hiker permits are first made available through a lottery in early spring. Apply between March 1 and March 31 through recreation.gov for a group of up to six people; results are announced in early April. Alternatively, day hikers may enter a daily permit lottery two days ahead of a planned climbing date, between midnight and 1 p.m., for about 50 permits available each day. About 23 percent of lottery entries succeed, with better percentages for weekdays and lower numbers for weekends. There's a fee to enter either lottery, and for those who win the right to buy permits, an additional per-hiker fee applies.

Backpackers apply separately. All overnight backcountry travelers need wilderness permits, which are available by reservation up to twenty-four weeks in advance through fax, phone, or mail. Check the Half Dome box on your request form. A fee is charged for reserved permits (per group request), plus an additional fee per group member. If granted, the Half Dome permits cost an additional fee per group member. Yosemite sets aside 50 of 75 daily Half Dome backpacker permits for those with advance reservations. See details at the nps.gov page for Yosemite wilderness permits.

Backpackers without reservations may request wilderness permits and Half Dome permits at the park's wilderness centers starting at 11 a.m. one day prior to their planned departure. There is currently no charge for no-reservation wilderness permits, though popular trailheads book up quickly. However, backpackers pay a per-person fee for Half Dome permits if they are available, just as day hikers do.

Yosemite sets aside 25 daily Half Dome backpacker permits for walk-up visitors.

Half Dome permits are nontransferable, and a ranger will check photo identification on the subdome, below the cables.

CLIMBING THE MOUNTAIN

Cross Happy Isles Bridge over Merced River before starting up the John Muir Trail. Crossing Vernal Fall Bridge, you'll arrive at a junction between the Mist and John Muir Trails. Most turn left onto the Mist Trail to get up close and personal with Vernal Fall. You could also turn right onto the Muir to avoid getting soaked.

Both trails cross bridges over Merced River and climb steeply. The paths reconnect just above Nevada Fall. Soon you'll reach another junction. To the right is the popular backpacking campground in Little Yosemite Valley; this is where you want to make camp on an overnight trip. If you're going straight to Half Dome, turn left.

After about 2 miles and 1,000 feet of elevation gain, turn left to leave the Muir and ascend Half Dome Trail.

A ranger will likely meet you beneath the subdome; check in and show your permit. Then climb about 600 steps to gain the mountain's shoulder and the base of the cables. Here comes the crux: a steep climb up about 200 yards on Half Dome's northeast face. Take a last look for dark clouds, and if any threaten, go back! Lightning can make the summit a death trap, so make a good decision and don't worry about "wasting" your

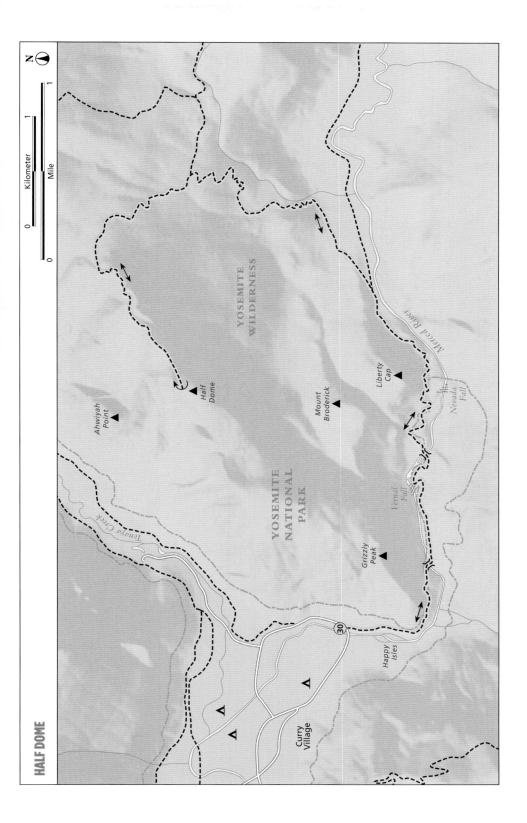

HALF DOME

permit. But if skies are clear, put on your gloves and muscle your way up. Enjoy your stay atop the most iconic mountain in the park.

HISTORY

Ahwahneechee called the mountain *Tis-si-ak*, after an Indian woman of legend; on its steepest side facing the valley, they saw her face and her tears. Josiah Whitney declared the summit "perfectly inaccessible," but George Anderson (1839–1884) made the first known ascent on October 12, 1875, drilling holes in the granite to insert bolts. Having difficulty keeping his footing in boots, he climbed his bolts without them and reached the top barefoot! Workers installed the cables in 1919.

MILES AND DIRECTIONS

0.0   At Happy Isles, hike south and then east on John Muir Trail

0.9   Cross Vernal Fall Bridge and continue hiking east on Mist Trail

1.0   At John Muir Trail junction, stay left (east) on Mist Trail

1.6   Reach Vernal Fall and hike east beside Merced River

4.1   Stay left (northeast) at Little Yosemite Valley trail junction

6.0   Go left (northwest) at Half Dome trail junction

8.1   Check the sky for clouds, summon your strength, and climb the cables

8.2   Summit

16.4 Arrive back at the trailhead

BONUS PEAKS IN YOSEMITE

MOUNT WATKINS

Elevation: 8,490 feet   **Difficulty:** Moderate

An adventure takes hikers to a fine summit with excellent views of Tenaya Canyon. Native Americans called the mountain *Waijau*, meaning "Pine Mountain." Today its official name honors photographer Carleton Watkins (1829–1916), who took some of the first pictures in Yosemite. The distance and mild elevation change could be called easy, although this outing does involve off-trail navigation. Park in a large pullout beside Tioga Road about 2 miles west of Olmsted Point. Cross the road and hike the southbound trail past a quarry for about a mile, until it veers right (west). Leave the summer trail here and continue hiking downhill to the south on the east slope of the ridge, following winter trail markers. Your route crosses a saddle and another established trail, which you should not take. Instead, ascend the north slope of Mount Watkins. The 5-mile round-trip outing requires only a few hundred feet of elevation change and takes three to five hours. Conditions are best from June through November.

RAGGED PEAK

Elevation: 10,912 feet   **Difficulty:** Moderate

A little-visited mountain near Tuolumne Meadows works as a day trip or overnight outing (permit required). Park at Lembert Dome and hike north toward Young Lakes. Reach the flank Ragged Peak in about 5 miles, leave the trail, and climb northeast to the saddle east of the peak. A Class 2–3 scramble leads to the summit. This 10-mile round-trip outing with 2,400 feet of elevation gain takes five to seven hours, and offers best conditions from June through October.

TENAYA PEAK

Elevation: 10,331 feet   **Difficulty:** Strenuous

This mountain's name honors Chief Tenaya of the Ahwahneechee; the Mariposa Battalion captured him here. Its proximity to Tioga Road and dramatic profile make this adventure appealing, yet its route finding and terrain pose challenges. The shortest way to its summit starts from the parking lot east of Tenaya Lake. From here, hike to the beach, cross Tenaya Creek (which might be tough in the early season), and hike the trail leading southwest beside the lake. Traverse up the west face (with Class 2 and 3 terrain) to the southwest ridge. Follow use trails to the summit. This is the route most technical climbers use to descend. The 3.5-mile round-trip gains 2,165 feet, involves potentially challenging route finding, and takes three to five hours. Others approach via Mildred Lake, which requires more hiking but less difficult climbing and scrambling. Conditions are best from June through October.

Kings Canyon aptly describes the gorge through its namesake national park.

KINGS CANYON AND SEQUOIA NATIONAL PARKS

Before thousands of climbers ascended Mount Whitney every year, a group of Buffalo Soldiers reached the summit in 1903. While today's climbers hike about 10 miles to top the high peak, the soldiers completed a rugged trek of 75 miles. They were the first African Americans to climb the mountain, and they built the first trail to its summit. Captain Charles Young described the scenery as the grandest he had ever seen.

"Indeed, a journey through this park and the Sierra Forest Reserve to the Mount Whitney country will convince even the least thoughtful man of the needfulness of preserving these mountains just as they are," wrote Young.

Under Young's command, Buffalo Soldiers protected Sequoia National Park's big trees, guarded against poachers and illegal grazing, and built more road in one summer than other troops had in the previous three combined.

Young wrote of a future in which "overworked and weary citizens of the country can find rest" in the park, "where wild scenic beauty cannot be surpassed." The Buffalo Soldiers' service and the contributions of many made that vision a reality.

GEOLOGY

Like the Sierra Nevada range as a whole, Sequoia and Kings Canyon and their surrounding forestlands rise gradually from the west. Glaciers and rivers carved deep canyons that descend toward the Central Valley; Kings Canyon National Park takes its name from such a valley, more than a mile deep.

Mountains tower much more steeply over the lands below in the east, where high peaks stand more than 10,000 feet higher than nearby Owens Valley. Twelve of California's fifteen mountains higher than 14,000 feet pierce the sky here, including Mount Whitney, the highest peak in the Lower 48.

Granitic rocks such as granite, diorite, and monzonite are common, as in much of the range. The parks also contain smaller amounts of volcanic and metamorphic rock, such as quartzite, phyllite, and marble.

Compared to Gold Rush hotbeds farther north, miners had little success here, except in Mineral King Valley, where prospectors unearthed silver from 1872 to 1881. However, spelunkers have discovered at least 275 caves, many more than a mile long and one extending 17 miles, the longest in California. Explorers find new caves every year, some containing bats, fossils, rare minerals, and beautiful formations. Crystal Cave in Sequoia and Boyden Cavern in Kings Canyon offer guided tours.

HISTORY

Native American history in the Southern Sierra dates back at least 6,000 years. Tribes included the Yokuts from west of the range. They created trans-Sierra paths that allowed them to trade and interact with Paiute to the east. The name *sequoia* itself honors a

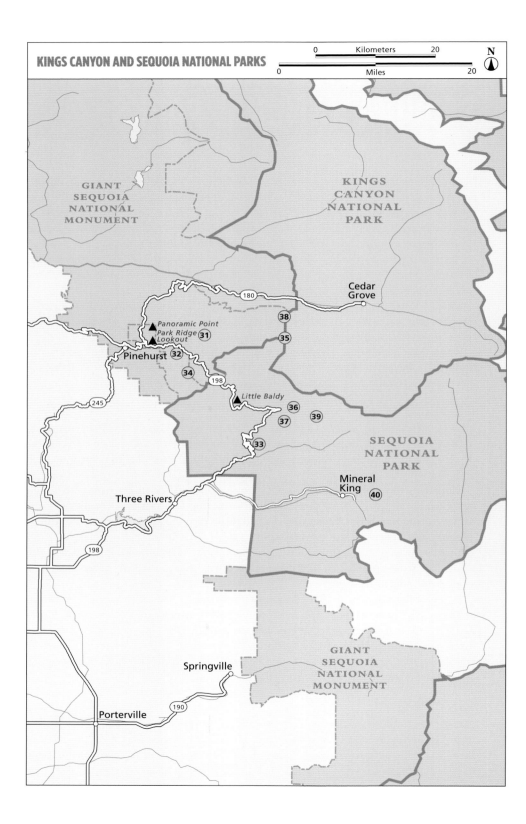

0　　　　Kilometers　　　20

0　　　　Miles　　　20

N

GIANT
SEQUOIA
NATIONAL
MONUMENT

KINGS
CANYON
NATIONAL
PARK

Cedar
Grove

180

38

Panoramic Point
Park Ridge
Lookout　31

35

Pinehurst　32

34

198

245

Little Baldy

36

39

37

33

SEQUOIA
NATIONAL
PARK

Mineral
King　40

Three Rivers

198

Springville

GIANT
SEQUOIA
NATIONAL
MONUMENT

Porterville　190

Cherokee man who created a written version of his people's language. However, diseases introduced by European Americans decimated the populations of Native peoples.

With assistance from Yokuts, rancher Hale Tharp found the Giant Forest in 1858 while seeking grazing land. He built a cabin from a downed sequoia where he still lived in 1875 when John Muir arrived and marveled at the scene. "It seemed impossible that any other forest picture in the world could rival it," wrote Muir. "Up spring the mighty walls of verdure three hundred feet high . . . every tree seemed religious and conscious of the presence of God."

Giant Forest shelters some 8,000 sequoias and most of the largest and oldest trees on Earth.

Of course loggers found the big trees too, built roads to reach them, and opened sawmills to harvest them. Starting in the 1860s, they felled thousands, including about a third of the sequoias, even though their brittle wood makes poor lumber. A group of utopian socialists formed the Kaweah Colony in 1886 and started work on a road to Giant Forest. There they discovered a sequoia so magnificent that they named it the Karl Marx Tree.

Citizens rallied to the trees' defense. Visalia newspaper editor George Stewart wrote his first of many editorials in support of preserving sequoias in 1878. Muir lent his voice and pen to the cause as well. Years of effort paid off when Congress declared Sequoia National Park and the more northern General Grant National Park open in 1890, much to the dismay of loggers like the Kaweah socialists. The government renamed the Karl Marx Tree, calling it instead the General Sherman Tree, after the Civil War Union leader.

But the struggle did not end there. Sequoia's original boundaries did not include the high country east of the big trees. Susan Thew, a forty-year-old Ohio transplant, resolved to change that. "I know of no better place than the wild loveliness of some chosen spot in the High Sierra in which, when you have lost your physical self, you have found your mental and spiritual re-awakening," she wrote. Thew journeyed hundreds of miles through the backcountry, producing a sixty-eight-page book that she submitted to Congress in 1926. Lawmakers had earlier rejected several expansion proposals, but after reviewing Thew's unprecedented photography, extended the boundary to the Sierra crest.

Superintendent John White sparred with developers for years. White arrived in 1920 when 28,000 visitors entered the park. By 1927, that figure had grown to 90,000. Ecologists realized human trampling over shallow roots harmed sequoias and prevented new ones from sprouting. Thus began White's crusade. "To preserve the national park atmosphere we must curb the human desire to develop the parks quickly to compete in popularity with other resorts," wrote White, who served for twenty-seven years. Sequoia's concessions company proposed additional cabins in 1931. White refused, and instead called for removing buildings from Giant Forest. The National Park Service overruled him, but White succeeded in limiting construction's destructive impacts.

General Grant National Park originally included only the sequoia grove named after the Civil War Union commander. Following Thew's example, photographer Ansel Adams captured images of deep canyons and high mountains to the east. Once again, dramatic photography succeeded where words had failed. Fifty years after creating General Grant National Park, Congress expanded it, renaming it Kings Canyon National Park in 1940. Sequoia and Kings Canyon remain closely connected today—by the 32-mile Generals Highway between them, and by the single park administration that has governed both since 1943.

Sierra, Sequoia, and Inyo National Forests protect much of the area between and around the two parks. Once coveted by Walt Disney for a proposed ski resort, Mineral King Valley instead became part of Sequoia National Park in 1978. White's vision of a more-natural and better-protected Giant Forest came to pass in the 1990s, when the park removed 282 buildings and restored 232 acres, moving commercial activity and lodging elsewhere. President Bill Clinton designated Giant Sequoia National Monument in 2000.

However, air pollution hurts visibility and the ecosystem, providing an ongoing challenge. In addition, warming temperatures, drought, and bark beetles killed more than 100 million California trees from 2010 through 2016, mostly in the Southern Sierra. Fortunately, a heavy winter slowed this trend in 2017, and scientists hope the survivors will fare better with fewer trees competing for water.

Today mountains carry the names of those who helped save these parks, like Muir and Stewart. Walter Fry Nature Center honors a reformed sequoia logger who became a guide, ranger, and superintendent. And trees credit the names of others, like Superintendent James Parker and President Abraham Lincoln.

Before the Buffalo Soldiers departed Sequoia in 1903, their commander also named a tree for "that great and good American, Booker T. Washington." Though a restaurant in nearby Visalia refused to serve the officer who was born a slave in 1864, Charles Young wrote that he longed to return to the big trees and tall mountains as he served his country around the world, and rose in rank to colonel.

A century later, with his tearful great-grandchildren present, the park named the Colonel Young Tree for its first African-American superintendent, one of many environmental heroes who left a mountain-sized legacy here.

VISITOR INFORMATION

Kings Canyon and Sequoia National Parks provide fantastic adventure opportunities with much less crowding and traffic than Yosemite experiences. The parks combined get less than half the number of visitors who enter their popular northern neighbor each year.

A single per-car, per-week fee allows you to enter both Kings Canyon and Sequoia National Parks. You can also purchase an annual pass to all national parks and monuments.

Wilderness permits are available at Foothills Visitor Center, Giant Forest Museum, and Kings Canyon Visitor Center year-round, and at Lodgepole, Cedar Grove, and Mineral King offices in summers only.

The Generals Highway between the parks closes in winter, as do Highway 180 to Cedar Grove, Mineral King Road, and the high country's forest roads.

31. **BUCK ROCK**

Home of a fire lookout for more than 100 years, this peak presents an easy outing that's perfect for families or those new to climbing. Favorable road conditions and a high-clearance vehicle can make the outing a short 0.5 mile round-trip, but many longer variations are possible. Experienced climbers will enjoy the summit's view and history, and cyclists and snow trekkers will find interesting opportunities too.

Distance: 10.4 miles round-trip (all on dirt roads), or much less! (See below)
Time: 1 to 5 hours; it depends! (See below)
Difficulty: Class 1; easy

Parking: Generals Highway/Big Meadows Road intersection
Trailhead elevation: 7,539 feet
Summit elevation: 8,502 feet
Elevation gain: 963 feet
Best season: June–Oct
Permits: None needed

FINDING THE TRAILHEAD

We start at the intersection of Generals Highway and Big Meadows Road, which meet on the border of Kings Canyon National Park and Giant Sequoia National Monument. If approaching from Kings Canyon National Park, drive about 6.5 miles southeast from the Y intersection of Highways 180 and 198. From the south, drive north and then west past the turnoff for Montecito Sequoia Lodge for 1 mile. Big Meadows Road leads to the north. The road closes each winter and reopens when snows recede, so summer and fall visitors can normally drive 2 or more miles closer to Buck Rock. GPS: N36 41.894' / W118 52.582'

CLIMBING THE MOUNTAIN

Follow Big Meadows Road (also labeled 14S11 on some maps) as it leads north and east for 2.8 miles. Then turn left (north) onto 13S04. Here the road becomes unpaved, winding, and rough; if you're still driving, consider parking and self-propelling the rest of the way. Continue as the road turns in a clockwise direction, climbing atop a northeast-bound ridge as the fire lookout comes into view. A sign marks the left (north) turn toward the summit block.

Staffed by Forest Service employees and volunteers, Buck Rock Fire Lookout opens to the public from 10 a.m. to 5 p.m. daily during fire season. As you enjoy the panoramic view of two national parks, a national monument, and millions of acres of pristine wilderness, give a thought to the hundreds of people who staffed this station to protect all that you see.

HISTORY

Native Americans called the peak "Finger Rock." Fire spotters used this perch as early as 1908, climbing a tree trunk to reach it. Forest workers constructed the building in

Buck Rock

Buck McGee, the station's first fire watcher, apparently did not inspire the name of the summit. Some believe that the profile of the rock resembles the face of a male Indian warrior, and other Americans once used the word *bucks* to refer to such men; hence, the name.

Prior to the installation of a phone in 1914, early fire spotters would descend and race to the site of fires by horseback. The lookout relied on gas and wood for much of the twentieth century, before electricity reached the building in the 1980s.

Wuksachi people once lived here during summer months, and have returned in recent years when Tribal elder Eddie Tupishna delivered an annual "Blessing of the Rock."

Sorry to Sequoia National Park skiers: Although this is an excellent winter trek, Generals Highway closes in winter, cutting off automobile access from the south.

1923, and 172 stairs replaced rickety wooden ladders in 1942. Buck McGee, the first fire watcher, staffed the lookout for several years in the 1920s. Leatrice Dotters, the first woman stationed there, followed in 1944.

Buck Rock looks over Giant Sequoia
National Monument.

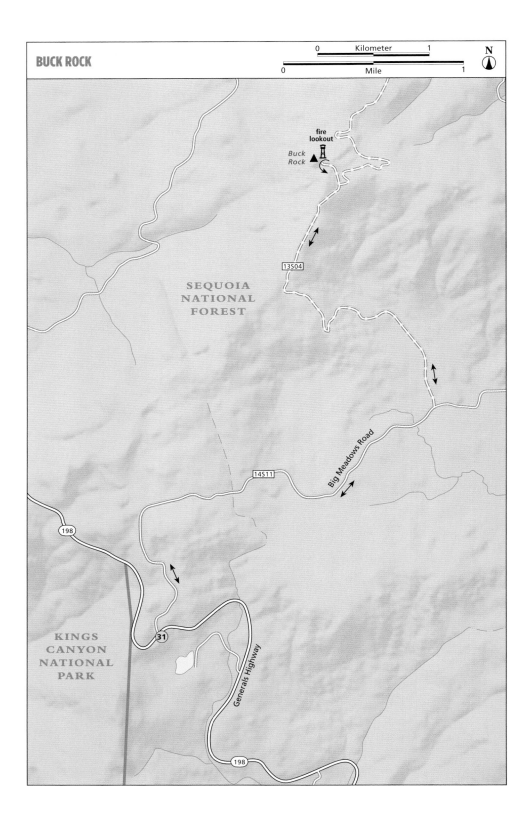

Kilometer

Mile

N

fire
lookout

*Buck
Rock*

13S04

SEQUOIA
NATIONAL
FOREST

14S11

Big Meadows Road

198

KINGS
CANYON
NATIONAL
PARK

31

Generals Highway

198

MILES AND DIRECTIONS

0.0 Hike (or bike, ski, or drive) northeast from Generals Highway onto Big Meadows Road/14S11

2.8 Turn left (north) onto 13S04

3.5 Stay left (west) on 13S04

4.1 Turn right (northwest) to stay on 13S04

5.0 Turn left (north) toward the summit

5.2 Summit

10.4 Arrive back at the trailhead

32. BUENA VISTA PEAK

A short and pleasant path achieves a marvelous vista of Redwood Mountain Canyon, Redwood Mountain, and distant High Sierra Peaks. This makes an excellent first summit for young children and climbers young at heart. There's no better payoff for such an easy climb in these parts, and no better introduction to Kings Canyon National Park.

Distance: 2 miles round-trip (all on trails)	**Trailhead elevation:** 7,176 feet
Time: 1 to 2 hours	**Summit elevation:** 7,587 feet
Difficulty: Class 1; easy	**Elevation gain:** 411 feet
Parking: Buena Vista Peak trailhead lot	**Best season:** May–Nov
	Permits: None needed

FINDING THE TRAILHEAD

Park at the signed Buena Vista Peak trailhead lot on Generals Highway, about 500 feet south of the Kings Canyon Overlook. GPS: N36 43.094' / W118 53.810'

CLIMBING THE MOUNTAIN

Hike west and then south on the clear trail past jeffrey pines, incense cedars, and large granite boulders. Soon the trail climbs above most trees and into better visibility. Where the trail crosses granite and becomes harder to follow, look for cairns to guide your way.

Our route curves slightly east as the summit comes into view; it's more of a dome than a peak. Beware of false use trails leading directly to its steep north-facing slope. Our path curves in a clockwise turn to climb its gentlest southeast slope.

Buck Rock Fire Lookout—constructed in 1923, and still staffed during fire season—may be visible to the northeast, as are many grand Sierra summits. This spot has particularly good views of Redwood Canyon and Redwood Mountain, home of the largest of all sequoia groves and the largest area of old-growth sequoia trees.

HISTORY

Ranger Sam Ellis (1860–1924) named this peak in 1895 in honor of its broad and majestic view of San Joaquin Valley. Ellis had reason to keep an eye

> ### SIERRA SECRETS
>
> This makes a fine winter outing for Kings Canyon National Park visitors, although it's important to remember that snow will cover the trail and require a measure of navigational know-how. Aim for the southeast slope, which provides the gentlest line to the summit. Unfortunately for Sequoia National Park skiers, you can't get there from here. Generals Highway closes in winter, cutting off automobile access from the south.
>
> Nearby Redwood Canyon has a variety of fine trails that see much less traffic than other Kings Canyon paths.

Buena Vista Peak

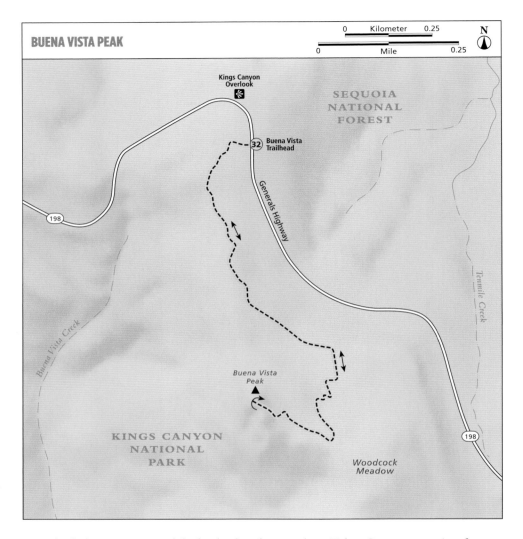

BUENA VISTA PEAK

Kings Canyon Overlook

SEQUOIA NATIONAL FOREST

32 Buena Vista Trailhead

Generals Highway

198

Buena Vista Creek

Tenmile Creek

Buena Vista Peak

KINGS CANYON NATIONAL PARK

Woodcock Meadow

198

on both the mountains and the lowlands, as he served as a Tulare County supervisor from 1890 to 1898. He's also known for serving on a posse and killing a murderer on the run in 1889.

MILES AND DIRECTIONS

0.0   Hike west from Buena Vista Peak trailhead

1.0   Summit

2.0   Arrive back at the trailhead

33. **MORO ROCK**

A short approach, stairs, and safety rails lead the way to the top of this granite dome. Steep cliffs and world-class panoramic views make it look and feel like a much bigger mountain, explaining its great popularity.

Distance: 0.4 mile round-trip (all on trails)
Time: 1 hour or less
Difficulty: Class 1; easy
Parking: Moro Rock trailhead lot or Giant Forest Museum lot

Trailhead elevation: 6,457 feet
Summit elevation: 6,725 feet
Elevation gain: 268 feet
Best season: April–Nov
Permits: None needed

FINDING THE TRAILHEAD

 Visitors can drive directly to Moro Rock's small parking area daily during shoulder seasons and on summer weekdays. Visitors must walk or take a free shuttle from Giant Forest Museum during summer weekends, when Moro Rock/Crescent Meadow Road closes to private automobiles. GPS: N36 32.811' / W118 45.939'

CLIMBING THE MOUNTAIN

Hike south on the paved path, climbing the first of about 400 steps. You will quickly rise above the surrounding trees as you reach the dome's northern base, where the grade becomes steeper. Soon you get a sense of high-altitude exposure as the narrow path leads above sheer drop-offs of more than 1,000 feet, but the paved stairs and steel safety rails give most climbers the courage to keep going.

> ### SIERRA SECRETS
>
> Enjoy this climb on summer weekdays or during the shoulder seasons; it gets crowded on summer weekends.
>
> Hiking from Giant Forest Museum to the summit trail adds 1.6 miles in each direction to the outing and provides a worthy alternative to waiting for shuttles on busy days.
>
> Moro Rock/Crescent Meadow Road closes to motor vehicles in winter when it becomes a snow trail. Skiers and snowshoers can approach and view the dome, but for safety reasons the park prohibits climbing its stairs when they are covered with snow or ice.
>
> The nearby Hanging Rock Trail provides excellent views of Moro Rock, adding about 0.25 mile in each direction.
>
> For best photography, visit during the afternoon (when the sun illuminates mountains to the east) and after rain (which improves air quality).
>
> Points of interest close to Crescent Meadow Road include a tunnel tree, Tharp's Log, and the Parker Group of Giant Sequoias.

Moro Rock

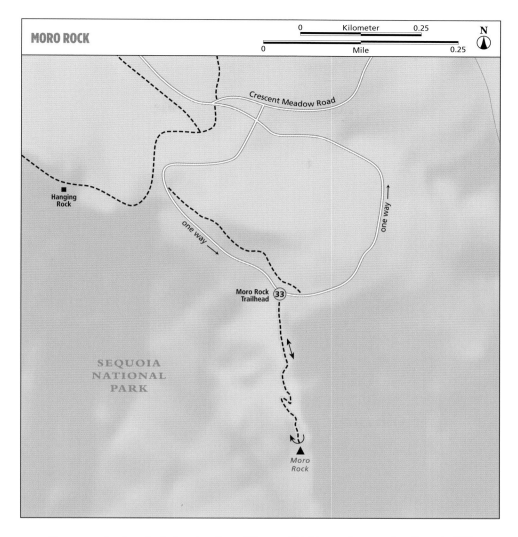

Hanging
Rock

Crescent Meadow Road

one way →

one way →

Moro Rock
Trailhead 33

SEQUOIA
NATIONAL
PARK

Moro
Rock

Our summit view includes the Great Western Divide to the east, San Joaquin Valley to the west, and conifer forests in all directions. "World-wide travelers, who have seen the best scenery of the Alps, the Andes, the Himalayas, and other mountain ranges, have declared the view from Moro Rock to be the equal of any," wrote Superintendent Walter Fry in 1931. Now you can judge for yourself.

HISTORY

A mustang of a bluish color, which Mexicans called a *moro*, made a habit of scrambling up, around, and under the ledges of this formation in the 1860s, so it became known as "Moro's Rock." Frontiersman Hale Tharp and his stepsons George Swanson (who owned the mustang) and John Swanson made the first known ascent in 1861. The National Park Service and the Civilian Conservation Corps built the stone stairway leading to the summit in the 1930s, replacing a rickety wooden staircase built in 1917.

Points of interest near Moro Rock include the Parker Group of Giant Sequoias.

MILES AND DIRECTIONS

0.0   Hike south from trailhead

0.2   Summit

0.4   Arrive back at the trailhead

34. BIG BALDY

This modest mountain that looks not unlike a bald hiker's head makes for a fine short sojourn in all seasons. The approach trail traces Big Baldy Ridge, which minimizes the elevation gain needed to achieve the summit. The route begins in a vibrant forest and ends on an exposed granite summit with excellent views in all directions.

Distance: 4.4 miles round-trip (all on trails)
Time: 2 to 3 hours
Difficulty: Class 1; easy to moderate
Parking: Beside Big Baldy trailhead

Trailhead elevation: 7,582 feet
Summit elevation: 8,209 feet
Elevation gain: 627 feet
Best season: June–Oct
Permits: None needed

FINDING THE TRAILHEAD

Park at the signed trailhead beside Generals Highway. If approaching from Kings Canyon National Park, drive about 6.5 miles southeast from the Y intersection of Highways 180 and 198. From the south, drive north and then west past the turnoff for Montecito Sequoia Lodge, for 1 mile. Find the parking and trailhead on the south side of the road at a sharp turn. GPS: N36 41.852' / W118 52.730'

CLIMBING THE MOUNTAIN

Our trail leads south past firs, pines, and boulders, tracing the border of Kings Canyon National Park and Giant Sequoia National Monument. Climbing gently, the route moves in and out of forest cover as views continually improve. Disregard two eastbound connecting trails that lead to Montecito Sequoia Lodge (which is private property). Some hikers stop at a nice vista about a 0.5 mile short of the peak, but if you're after the true summit, keep going, because you're almost there.

From the top, we see Redwood Canyon and Redwood Mountain Grove to the west and the High Sierra peaks of the Great Western Divide to the east.

HISTORY

Members of the California Geological Survey ascended the mountain in June 1864, observing that its "summit is smooth and bare and reflects the sun's rays," and noting

SIERRA SECRETS

Our trail continues south past the summit and offers views of Chimney Rock and Little Baldy, though the less-maintained route becomes more rugged and includes Class 2 and 3 terrain.

While this trip makes a fine ski/snowshoe outing for those approaching from Kings Canyon National Park, Generals Highway closes in winter, which makes the trailhead inaccessible by car from Sequoia National Park.

For best visibility, hike to this summit after rainfall, which improves air quality.

Guests at Montecito Sequoia Lodge can access this trail from the resort's westbound fire roads and connecting trails.

Big Baldy

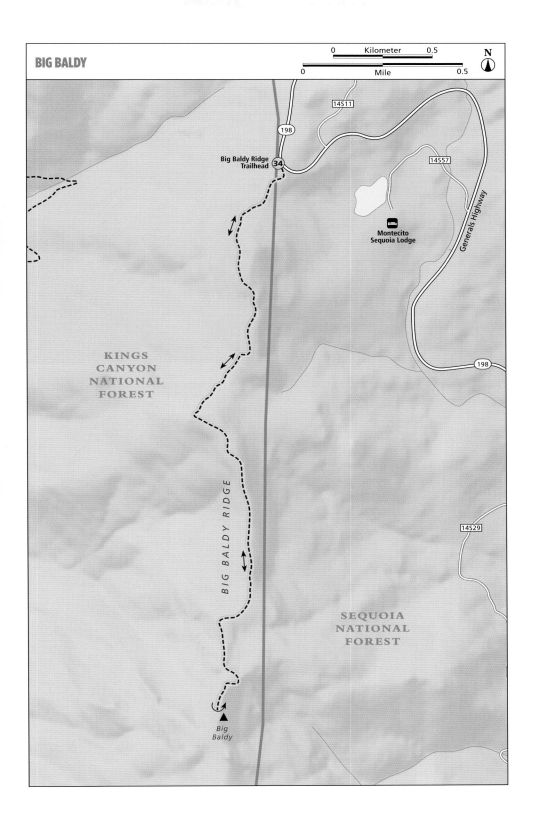

0   Kilometer   0.5

0   Mile   0.5

N

14511

198

Big Baldy Ridge
Trailhead   34

14557

Montecito
Sequoia Lodge

Generals Highway

198

KINGS
CANYON
NATIONAL
FOREST

BIG BALDY RIDGE

14S29

SEQUOIA
NATIONAL
FOREST

Big
Baldy

Summits of the Great Western Divide highlight the view to the east.

that it was "prominent from the valley floor throughout Tulare County." The name *Big Baldy* appeared on a 1905 map.

MILES AND DIRECTIONS

0.0   Hike south from Big Baldy trailhead

0.1   Stay right (south) at trail junction

1.0   Stay right (south) at trail junction

2.2   Summit

4.4   Arrive back at the trailhead

35. MITCHELL PEAK

Short and moderate by High Sierra standards, the hike atop Mitchell Peak affords visitors an incredible view of the mountains that ranks among the best in the entire range. Because of its somewhat remote trailhead, the route gets much less visitation than other popular hikes in the Sequoia and Kings Canyon area.

Distance: 5.8 miles round-trip (all on trails)
Time: 3 to 4 hours
Difficulty: Class 2; moderate (for distance and elevation gain)
Parking: Marvin Pass trailhead

Trailhead elevation: 8,200 feet
Summit elevation: 10,365 feet
Elevation gain: 2,165 feet
Best season: June–Oct
Permits: None needed

FINDING THE TRAILHEAD

Driving on Generals Highway north of Montecito Sequoia Lodge, look for a sign that reads "Big Meadows/Horse Corral Road." Turn northeast onto Big Meadows Road / FR 14S11 and drive 12 miles to the Sequoia High Sierra Camp/Marvin Pass turnoff. Turn right onto FR 13S12 and drive for another 2.5 miles to the parking area. GPS: N36 44.447' / W118 44.287'

CLIMBING THE MOUNTAIN

Our hike begins with a steady climb south for about a mile to Marvin Pass. Enjoy the sea of conifers in Sequoia National Forest and pass into Jennie Lakes Wilderness. At the signed junction, turn left toward Mitchell Peak.

Now the route borders a lush green meadow that might provide your best view of Mitchell Peak itself. Look for wildflowers, including lupine, skyrockets, and snow plants. Follow the trail toward Kanawyer Gap, but turn left again at the next signed junction.

SIERRA SECRETS

This summit borders Jennie Lakes Wilderness, Kings Canyon National Park, and Giant Sequoia National Monument, created by President Bill Clinton in 2000.

While leashed dogs are legal on hikes in Sequoia National Forest (including Jennie Lakes Wilderness and Giant Sequoia National Monument), they are not allowed on trails in the surrounding Kings Canyon and Sequoia National Parks.

Mitchell Peak's view is so broad and encompassing that the summit once housed a fire lookout station.

Sequoia High Sierra Camp, located about a mile east of the parking lot, offers lodging and meals.

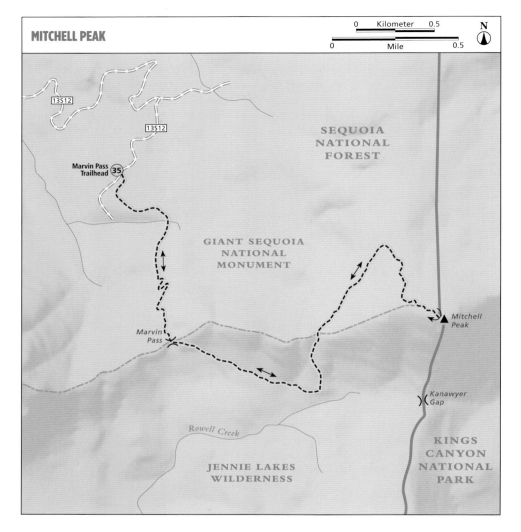

Your final approach takes you above the tree line to the giant boulder pile that marks the summit. Watch your step as you navigate the rocks. From the peak, gaze upon the 360-degree view of trees, valleys, and distant snowcapped summits.

HISTORY

The peak's name honors Susman Mitchell (1859–1934), a Visalia postmaster and banker who once scaled Mount Whitney and helped form a climbers' club in 1901. Sam Ellis of the Sierra Forest Preserve named nearby Jennie Lake for his wife in 1897, a name later applied to the surrounding Jennie Lakes Wilderness.

MILES AND DIRECTIONS

0.0   Hike south and uphill through the forest toward Marvin Pass

0.6   Stay left (south) at trail junction

1.0   Turn left (east) at Marvin Pass

1.6   Turn left (north) at trail junction

2.9   Summit

5.8   Arrive back at the trailhead

36. THE WATCHTOWER

This moderate outing leads through a vibrant forest to a dramatic and fascinating mountaintop at the edge of a beautiful and popular cluster of backcountry lakes.

Distance: 6.6 miles round-trip (on trails with some rock scrambling)	**Trailhead elevation:** 7,280 feet
Time: 3 to 4 hours	**Summit elevation:** 8,973 feet
Difficulty: Class 2; moderate (for distance and elevation gain)	**Elevation gain:** 1,693 feet
	Best season: June–Oct
Parking: Wolverton Picnic Area lot	**Permits:** None needed

FINDING THE TRAILHEAD

From Generals Highway in Sequoia National Park, turn northeast onto Wolverton Road and drive about 1.5 miles to Wolverton Picnic Area. GPS: N36 35.830' / W118 44.075'

CLIMBING THE MOUNTAIN

Hike north from the parking lot to a trail junction. Turn right to stay on Lakes Trail. Hike east beside Wolverton Creek on the path through a forest of pines and firs. Turn left (north) at the next trail junction, toward Heather Lake and Pear Lake. Now the climbing becomes steeper. Our next junction offers a choice of The Watchtower Trail or The Hump Trail; stay left for The Watchtower. From here to the peak is another 1.3 miles, crossing seasonal creeks. Look for corn lilies, ranger buttons, and columbine wildflowers on the way.

Watchtower's granite summit stands across a chasm north of the trail. Most passersby are content to admire it from the trailside. Some scamper up Class 2 terrain on its southwest flank, but be advised that its north and east faces drop more than 1,000 feet, with no fencing or rails. Parents beware: Although many children hike this trail, the summit

SIERRA SECRETS

Both Tokopah Falls and Tokopah Valley get their names from a Yokut term for "high mountain valley."

To make a longer trip and a loop, return via Heather Lake and The Hump Trail for a total distance of about 8 miles. This way you'll get to see the most dramatic portion of the trail (between The Watchtower and Heather Lake), where CCC workers blasted into the solid granite of the mountainside.

If you wish to camp, excellent sites are found beside Emerald and Pear Lakes (permit required). There is no camping allowed at Aster or Heather Lakes.

Although Wolverton is a popular winter recreation area, the park closes The Watchtower Trail when icy or snowed over for safety reasons.

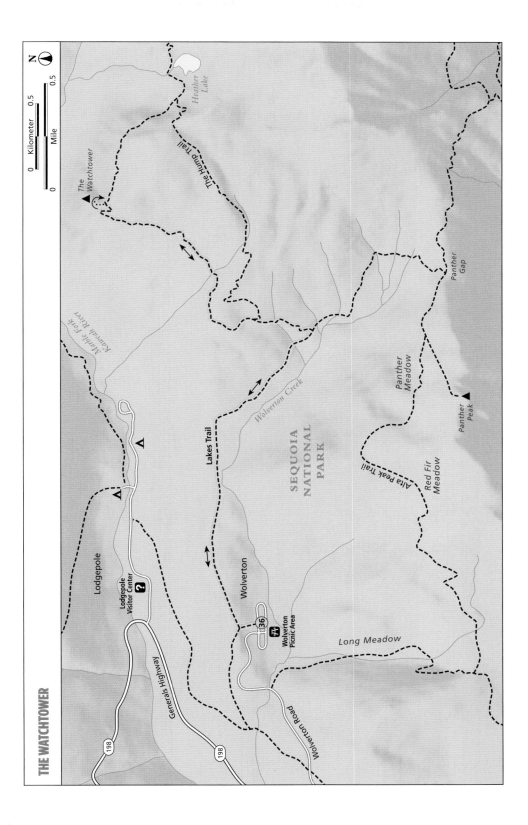

THE WATCHTOWER

is no place for kids. Admire Tokopah Valley and the Marble Fork of the Kaweah River to the north.

HISTORY

This mountain's steep and pointy appearance as seen from Tokopah Falls inspired its informal name; most maps do not identify it except as an unnamed 8,973-foot peak. More than 1,100 members of FDR's Civilian Conservation Corps worked in and around Sequoia National Park starting in 1933. Some of them camped at nearby Emerald Lake while working on this trail, earning $1 a day each for their labor.

MILES AND DIRECTIONS

0.0   Hike north on Lakes Trail

0.1   Turn right (east) at junction to stay on Lakes Trail

1.7   Turn left (north) at junction toward Heather Lake and Pear Lake

2.0   Stay left (north) for The Watchtower Trail

3.3   Summit

6.6   Arrive back at the trailhead

37. PANTHER PEAK

A moderate hike reaches an inspiring view of a grand river canyon and the Great Western Divide. This outing starts on a popular trail but becomes less populated the farther hikers go, and you will probably have the summit to yourself.

Distance: 6.6 miles round-trip (on trails and cross-country)
Time: 3 to 4 hours
Difficulty: Class 2; moderate (for distance and off-trail travel)
Parking: Wolverton Picnic Area lot

Trailhead elevation: 7,280 feet
Summit elevation: 9,046 feet
Elevation gain: 1,766 feet
Best season: June–Oct
Permits: None needed

FINDING THE TRAILHEAD

From Generals Highway in Sequoia National Park, turn northeast onto Wolverton Road and drive about 1.5 miles to Wolverton Picnic Area. GPS: N36 35.792' / W118 44.063'

CLIMBING THE MOUNTAIN

Hike north from the parking lot to a trail junction. Turn right to stay on Lakes Trail. Follow the path beside Wolverton Creek to the east, climbing gradually through the forest of pines and firs. Stay right at the trail junction to stay on Lakes Trail (labeled "Panther Gap Trail" on some maps) as you cross several streams and contour south to Panther Gap. From here you can see our destination about a 0.5 mile to the west.

Turn right (west) onto Alta Peak Trail, but only for about 0.25 mile. The trail runs beside and beneath the mountain, and climbers should turn left off the trail and ascend through the forest to the summit (which will not be clearly visible). You may find a use trail, but if not, just keep going uphill to the southwest. Granite blocks and boulders crown the top; to reach their highest point requires a little scrambling.

Our view to the east is especially grand. Feast your eyes on the deep canyon

SIERRA SECRETS

Hikers can make this outing into a 7-mile loop by continuing west on Alta Peak Trail, turning north at Long Meadow and returning to Wolverton.

Panther Peak makes a great double with Alta Peak, although it sees much less visitation than its taller neighbor.

Castle Rocks look grand and appealing, but see even less visitation than Panther Peak because of the grueling off-trail hike required to reach them.

Mountain lions still populate the Sierra Nevada, though they are elusive and sightings are rare. Panther attacks in these mountains are rarer still, with just three documented incidents between 1994 and 2018. Rangers advise hikers who see a mountain lion to stand their ground, make loud noises, and throw rocks to scare the predator away.

Panther Peak

PANTHER PEAK

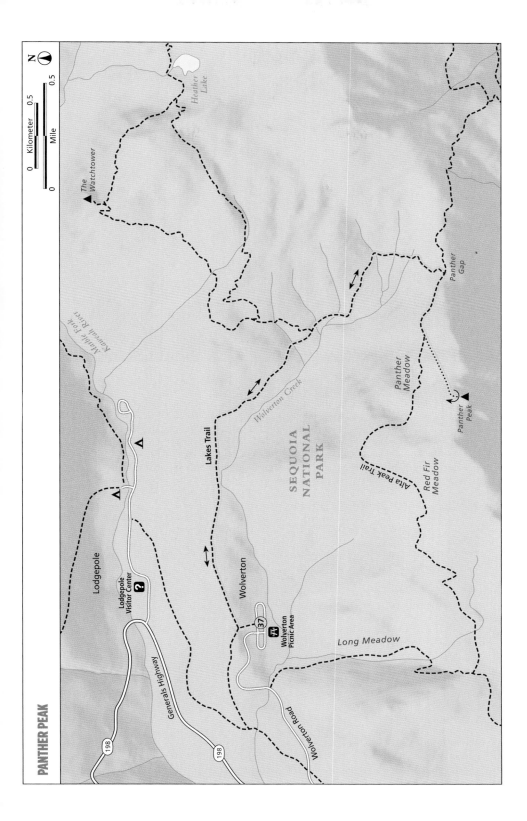

formed by the Middle Fork of the Kaweah River, the Castle Rocks above it, and distant High Sierra peaks.

HISTORY

After frontiersman Hale Tharp killed a mountain lion in this area, the nearby stream became known as Panther Creek, and the name Panther Peak appeared on maps by 1905.

MILES AND DIRECTIONS

- **0.0** Hike north on Lakes Trail
- **0.1** Turn right (east) at junction to stay on Lakes Trail
- **1.7** Stay right (southeast) at junction toward Alta Peak and Mehrten Meadow
- **2.6** Turn right (west) at Panther Gap onto Alta Peak Trail
- **2.8** Leave Alta Peak Trail and climb up to the left (southwest)
- **3.3** Summit
- **6.6** Arrive back at the trailhead

38. LOOKOUT PEAK

Lookout Peak rates as one of the more difficult climbs in this region, but rewards ambitious hikers with grand, sweeping views of Kings Canyon. So impressed with this vista was John Muir that he declared this area "a rival of the Yosemite."

Distance: 10.4 miles round-trip (all on trails)
Time: 5 to 7 hours
Difficulty: Class 3; strenuous (for distance, elevation gain, and summit scramble)

Parking: Near Cedar Grove
Trailhead elevation: 4,670 feet
Summit elevation: 8,531 feet
Elevation gain: 3,861 feet
Best season: May–Oct
Permits: None needed

FINDING THE TRAILHEAD

Park near Cedar Grove, either in a pullout beside Highway 180 or in a day-use lot. Find Don Cecil Trail leading south of the highway about 200 yards east of the highway's intersection with North Side Drive. GPS: N36 47.395' / W118 40.167'

CLIMBING THE MOUNTAIN

Start hiking the trail that soon crosses a dirt road leading to a heliport. Our path turns southwest as the climbing begins. This initial portion of Don Cecil Trail attracts many hikers bound for Sheep Creek Cascade, a short but pretty waterfall found 0.8 mile from the trailhead. Once you reach it and cross the footbridge over Sheep Creek, you will likely have the trail to yourself.

Ascend switchbacks as the trail climbs through ponderosa pines, cedars, and oaks. The climbing grows more difficult, but every step improves your view of the glacially carved Kings Canyon to the north.

> ### SIERRA SECRETS
>
> Don Cecil Trail, which leads from Cedar Grove to the mountain, is named for an 1800s shepherd. Long before paved roads allowed automobiles to enter Kings Canyon, this path provided access for visitors, including John Muir. "Here too we see the forest in broad dark swaths still sweeping onward undaunted, climbing the farther mountain-slopes to a height of 11,000 feet," wrote the naturalist.
>
> Highway 180 to Cedar Grove typically opens to automobiles in late April and closes with the first major snowfall in fall or winter. Get an early start on this one, and bring plenty of water to beat the heat.
>
> Seems like cheating, but suit yourself: Visitors could drive within a 0.5 mile of this summit using Big Meadows Road/FR 14S11. It's about 15 miles from the Generals Highway turnoff, with no guarantees about conditions on the dirt road. Mountain bikers can approach the peak this way, too.

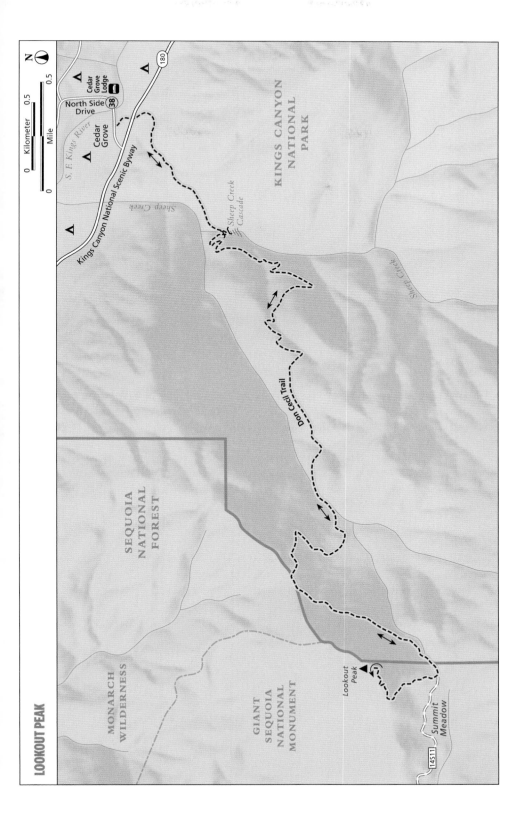

LOOKOUT PEAK

N

0   Kilometer   0.5

0   Mile   0.5

Kings Canyon National Scenic Byway

180

38   North Side Drive

Cedar Grove Lodge

Cedar Grove

S.F. Kings River

Sheep Creek

Sheep Creek Cascade

Sheep Creek

KINGS CANYON NATIONAL PARK

MONARCH WILDERNESS

SEQUOIA NATIONAL FOREST

GIANT SEQUOIA NATIONAL MONUMENT

Don Cecil Trail

Lookout Peak

Summit Meadow

14S11

Sheep Creek Cascade flows beside Don Cecil Trail.

Our path reaches a saddle just south of Lookout Peak and crosses FR 14S11 at the edge of Summit Meadow. Turn north to stay on Don Cecil Trail, which steepens, narrows, and climbs switchbacks up the mountain's southern slope.

Near the summit, hikers will reach curious radio transmitters. This is a good stopping point for many because the final portion of climbing requires Class 3 scrambling up the granite boulders above. But if you're prepared for that, climb on. Your summit view of Kings Canyon, Sequoia National Forest, Monarch Wilderness, and distant High Sierra peaks might soothe your sore muscles.

HISTORY

Elisha Winchell made the first known ascent on September 27, 1868, naming it "Winchell's Peak" for her cousin. Explorer Joseph LeConte later called it "Grand Lookout," and the current name first appeared on a 1905 map.

MILES AND DIRECTIONS

0.0   Hike south from the trailhead on Don Cecil Trail

0.8   Cross the footbridge above Sheep Creek Cascade

4.7   Turn right (north) to stay on Don Cecil Trail

5.2   Summit

10.4   Arrive back at the trailhead

39. ALTA PEAK

A long hike and abundant elevation gain make this peak a challenge, but that's why climbing it will feel so great. You will feel far away from the crowds surrounding popular attractions like General Sherman Tree when you stand atop this grand mountain overlooking Sequoia National Park.

Distance: 13.4 miles round-trip (all on trails)
Time: 6 to 8 hours
Difficulty: Class 2; strenuous (for distance and elevation gain)
Parking: Wolverton Picnic Area lot

Trailhead elevation: 7,280 feet
Summit elevation: 11,204 feet
Elevation gain: 3,924 feet
Best season: June–Oct
Permits: None needed

FINDING THE TRAILHEAD

From Generals Highway in Sequoia National Park, turn northeast onto Wolverton Road and drive about 1.5 miles to Wolverton Picnic Area. GPS: N36 35.795' / W118 44.063'

CLIMBING THE MOUNTAIN

Hike north from the parking lot and quickly reach a trail junction; turn right to stay on Lakes Trail. Our path leads east and gradually climbs through the forest and beside Wolverton Creek. Stay right at the next trail junction (hiking what some maps call Panther Gap Trail) as you cross several streams and contour south to Panther Gap. Once there, you will enjoy a broad and inspiring view of the deep canyon formed by the Middle Fork of the Kaweah River.

Turn left and east onto Alta Trail (shown on some maps as Alta Peak Trail) as it traces the north rim of the river canyon for a mile. Then at Mehrten Meadow, turn left at the trail junction to stay on Alta Trail; you don't want to turn right onto Sevenmile Trail, dropping steeply into the canyon. At the next junction, turn left again as you pass Tharps Rock. Be sure to appreciate the rare and rugged foxtail pines growing here, which can live longer than 2,000 years. The final approach is steep, physical, and worth every step. You'll understand why when

> ### SIERRA SECRETS
>
> Beware: Snow may cover trails on mountains this high well into the summer.
>
> Bag two summits in one day by adding Panther Peak to your agenda. Its summit stands only 0.5 miles from Panther Gap, making the total detour 1 mile, with about 500 feet of elevation gain.
>
> For those making an overnight trip, Mehrten Meadow makes a nice camping spot.
>
> In all of the Sierra Nevada mountains, foxtail pines grow only in the area of Kings Canyon and Sequoia National Parks.

Alta Peak

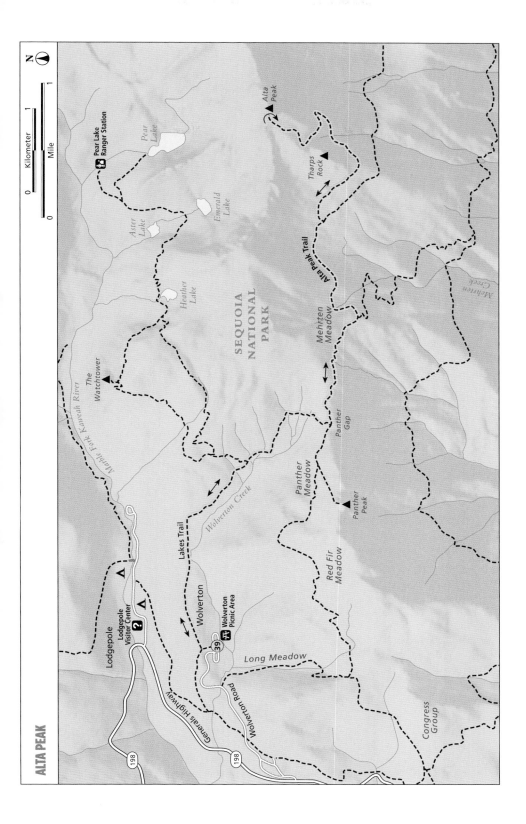

ALTA PEAK

SEQUOIA NATIONAL PARK

Pear Lake Ranger Station

Pear Lake

Aster Lake

Emerald Lake

Heather Lake

The Watchtower

Marble Fork Kaweah River

Lakes Trail

Wolverton Creek

Wolverton

Lodgepole

Lodgepole Visitor Center

Generals Highway

Wolverton Road

Wolverton Picnic Area

Long Meadow

Panther Meadow

Red Fir Meadow

Panther Peak

Panther Gap

Mehrten Meadow

Alta Peak Trail

Tharps Rock

Alta Peak

Mehrten Creek

Congress Group

198

39

N

0   Kilometer   1

0   Mile   1

Aster, Emerald, and Pear Lakes enhance the northern view.

you enjoy the breathtaking panoramic view from the summit. No wonder the bold and hungry marmots who live here don't want to leave!

HISTORY

This mountain was once called Tharps Peak after Hale Tharp, but settlers named the nearby Alta Meadow for its height, and the residents of Three Rivers came to use the name "Alta" for the peak as well. William Dudley made the first known ascent in 1896.

MILES AND DIRECTIONS

0.0   Hike north on Lakes Trail

0.1   Turn right (east) at junction to stay on Lakes Trail

1.7   Stay right (southeast) at junction toward Alta Peak and Mehrten Meadow

2.6   Turn left (east) at Panther Gap onto Alta Peak Trail

3.6   Turn left (northeast) at junction to stay on Alta Trail

4.6   Turn left (northeast) at junction to stay on Alta Trail

6.7   Summit

13.4 Arrive back at the trailhead

40. SAWTOOTH PEAK

A physical climb leads to a spectacular summit above the little-known Mineral King Valley of Sequoia National Park. A winding and narrow road deters most visitors, but those who brave the drive into this scenic wonderland won't soon forget it.

Distance: 12 miles round-trip (on trails and use trails with rock scrambling)
Time: 6 to 8 hours
Difficulty: Class 3; strenuous (for distance, elevation gain, and terrain)

Parking: Timber Gap trailhead
Trailhead elevation: 7,843 feet
Summit elevation: 12,343 feet
Elevation gain: 4,500 feet
Best season: June–Oct
Permits: None needed

FINDING THE TRAILHEAD

Motorists can access Mineral King Road from Highway 198 about 4 miles northeast of Three Rivers. The scenic but slow road takes more than an hour to drive, and closes each winter; park officials do not recommend RVs or trailers on this route. It's 25 miles to its end, and Timber Gap trailhead. GPS: N36 27.179' / W118 35.798'

CLIMBING THE MOUNTAIN

Hike north and then east from the trailhead. Climbing starts right away on switchbacks. Stay right when Timber Gap Trail splits from our Sawtooth Pass Trail. Cross Monarch Creek and then continue up switchbacks, passing through meadows, a red fir forest, and the avalanche-scored Chihuahua Bowl, named by hopeful miners after a prospecting area in Mexico.

Stay left at our next junction to stay on Sawtooth Pass Trail. Climbing eases as we clear 10,000 feet and contour around Mineral Peak to the lower of the Monarch Lakes.

Now our path leads up the long, sandy, and physically demanding slope to the north. This segment of the trail may be difficult to see, especially when covered by snow; aim for the saddle northwest of Sawtooth Peak. From the saddle, hike off-trail along the ridge leading to the jagged granite summit. The ridge contains Class 2 terrain, and then the final summit push features some Class 3 scrambling. Between the distance, elevation gain, and rock climbing, those who reach the top have certainly earned the outstanding panoramic view of the Southern Sierra.

Be careful to retrace your steps on the way back and resist the temptation to make a more-direct but perilously steep descent to Monarch Lakes.

HISTORY

Deer hunter Joseph Lovelace made the first known ascent in 1871. James Wright called the mountain "Miners' Peak," but also used the name "Saw Tooth" in 1881 writings. The latter name aptly describes the peak and its northwestern ridge's jagged edge, and caught on with locals of Mineral King during its mining boom of the 1870s. The current name first appeared on a 1904 map.

Sawtooth Peak

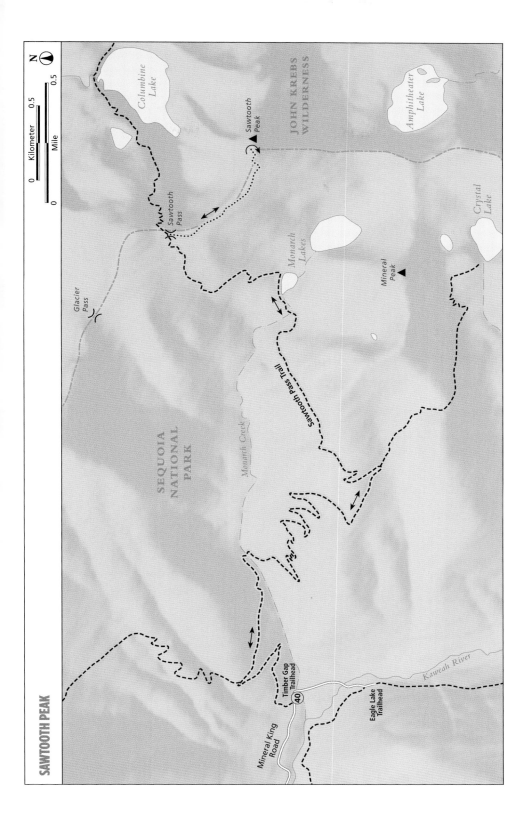

SAWTOOTH PEAK

Sawtooth Pass Trail passes right by Lower Monarch Lake, a scenic rest spot fit for royalty.

MILES AND DIRECTIONS

0.0 Hike north from Timber Gap trailhead

0.6 Stay right (east) on Sawtooth Pass Trail

3.2 Stay left (north) on Sawtooth Pass Trail

5.0 Turn right (southeast) to leave trail and follow ridge to summit

6.0 Summit

12.0 Arrive back at the trailhead

SIERRA SECRETS

Timber Gap trailhead has parking, but you might want to leave your vehicle in the lot across from Mineral King Ranger Station instead. That's because hungry marmots have been known to chew through automobile hoses and wires, sometimes "hitching" rides home with unsuspecting visitors, or even disabling their vehicles! This is why some motorists wrap their cars and trucks with tarps like giant birthday gifts. Rangers also suggest parking at lower elevations, like beside the ranger station, where marmots are less troublesome. Doing so will add 0.8 mile to your trip each way.

This hike passes through John Krebs Wilderness, designated in 2009 and named for the congressman who championed adding this area to Sequoia National Park. Krebs (1926–2014) served three terms in the House of Representatives and lost his last reelection effort in 1980, after fighting to preserve Mineral King Valley rather than allow extensive commercial development.

BONUS PEAKS IN KINGS CANYON AND SEQUOIA NATIONAL PARKS

PANORAMIC POINT

Elevation: 7,520 feet   **Difficulty:** Easy

There's no shorter hike to a better view in this book, or perhaps anywhere. Take Highway 180 to Grant Grove Village in Kings Canyon National Park. Turn east into the village, drive past the visitor center toward John Muir Lodge, and turn right (east) onto Panoramic Point Road (no RVs or trailers allowed). The road winds and climbs about 2 miles northeast to a parking area. A signed trail leads about 0.3 mile and gains 100 feet to the vista, which features a world-class view of Hume Lake and distant mountaintops. The total outing takes one hour or less. Conditions are best from June through October. Panoramic Point Road closes to automobiles in winter but remains open to skiers and snowshoers; the outing from the gate beside John Muir Lodge totals 4.6 miles round-trip.

PARK RIDGE LOOKOUT

Elevation: 7,540 feet   **Difficulty:** Moderate

If you liked Panoramic Point but want a longer outing, here's a slightly higher summit with a fire lookout available from the same trailhead. Take Highway 180 to Grant Grove Village in Kings Canyon National Park. Turn east into the village, right (east) onto Panoramic Point Road (no RVs or trailers allowed), and drive 2 miles to a parking area. Hike on Park Ridge Trail past Panoramic Point, continuing south for 2.5 additional miles. Along the way you will crest Park Ridge (7,776 feet) as an added bonus. The trail crosses a forest road that also leads to the lookout; you can take either one. Visitors are welcome in the lookout from 10 a.m. to 5 p.m. daily during fire season. The trip totals 6.1 miles round-trip, gains about 330 feet, and takes three to four hours. Conditions are best from June through October. This is another winter option for skiers and snowshoers, totaling 9.6 miles round-trip from John Muir Lodge.

LITTLE BALDY

Elevation: 8,044 feet   **Difficulty:** Moderate

Here's a short and sweet climb from a convenient trailhead to an excellent view in Sequoia National Park. Park beside Generals Highway at the signed Little Baldy Saddle, either 1.5 miles south of Dorst Creek Campground, or 2.8 miles north from Halstead Meadow Picnic Area. Pick up the trail on the east side of the road, leading northeast to switchbacks and then turning south. The path leads through a forest and then onto a granite dome. Our summit view includes features of the Great Western Divide to the east and Big Baldy to the north. You'll be surprised at how few people make this moderate hike with such a good payoff. The outing gains about 800 feet, totals 3.2 miles round-trip, and takes about two hours. Conditions are best from June through October.

Sharp peaks and sage typify the glorious Eastern Sierra landscape.

EASTERN SIERRA

Eastern Sierra's jagged peaks rise so sharply above Owens Valley that they can appear quite intimidating. So thought Mary Austin, a settler and future author who moved to the town of Lone Pine in 1892.

"Abruptly on the west rose the vast ghost-gray bulk of Opopago," she wrote, using the Paiute name for Lone Pine Peak, "and behind it Whitney towering to look down on Death Valley . . . Nothing saved the town from the sense of imminent disaster from that overhanging bulk but the backs of an ancient line of treeless hills called Alabama."

But the steep mountains grew on Austin, who hiked and camped among them many times during the fifteen years she lived in their shadow. Her affection for the range shows in her first book, *The Land of Little Rain,* in which she described the "thunder-splintered sierras" with reverence and awe: "When those glossy domes swim into the alpenglow, wet after rain, you conceive how long and imperturbable are the purposes of God."

GEOLOGY

Western and eastern sides of the Sierra Nevada range differ dramatically. While the western slope climbs gradually from the Central Valley to the crest, the far steeper eastern slope stands like a wall over the lands below. Why the difference? The mountain range is a block of the Earth's crust with a major fault on its eastern side. Plate movement caused the east side of the range to rise sharply while the west side tilted more gently downward, groomed by west-bound streams and glaciers. Geologists believe much of this movement occurred in the last two million years. Today the range acts as a weather barrier, blocking most eastbound precipitation and making the lands east of the mountains desert-like and dry.

HISTORY

Indigenous people inhabited the lands beneath the Eastern Sierra mountains for millennia. Paiute who called the area *Payahüünadü* (place of flowing water) learned to irrigate crops long before European Americans renamed their home Owens Valley, and Shoshone thrived in a desert so inhospitable it was later named Death Valley.

Among the first European Americans to pass through the area was Joseph Walker, who led fifty-eight fur trappers west over the mountains in 1833. Theodore Talbot led a group that included Walker south through Owens Valley in 1845. Explorer John Fremont named the area for his guide, Richard Owens.

Ranchers, including Samuel Bishop, arrived near the city now named for him in 1861, raising cattle that supported miners in nearby Nevada. Encouraged by the Homestead Act of 1862, which offered settlers land (frequently occupied by Native Americans) for $1.25 per acre, more ranchers and farmers followed, building the towns that sprung up at Lone Pine, Independence, Lee Vining, and Bridgeport.

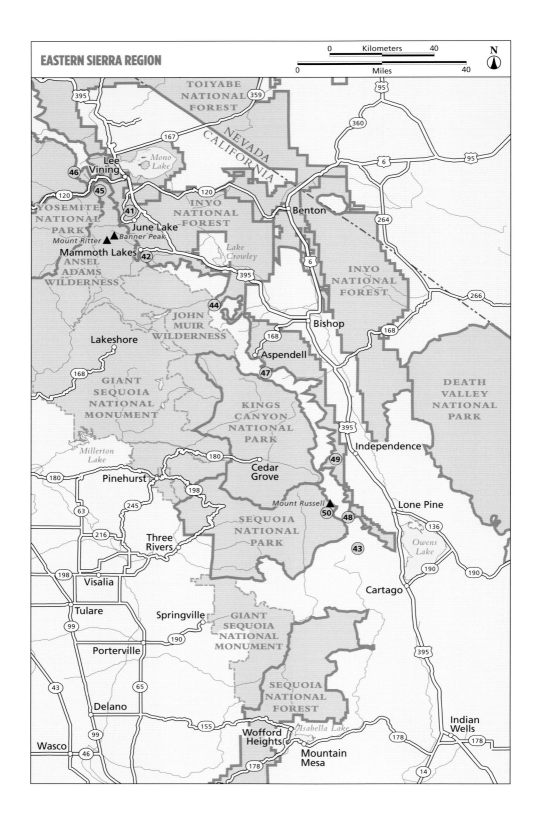

Ranchers and US Cavalry troops fought Paiute and Shoshone in 1862 and 1863. During the conflict European Americans killed about 200 Natives and forced survivors onto a reservation at Fort Tejon, 240 miles to the south. Native Americans now occupy several Eastern Sierra reservations. Paiute and Shoshone operate a cultural center in Bishop that honors more than 50 college graduates and more than 150 veterans. Among them are Jeff Yandell, James Warlie, and Richard Watson, who all served in World War I, and Richard Charley and Karen Manuelito, who both served in the Iraq War. Among those who have labored to preserve their culture are Kathy Bancroft, Alan Spoonhunter, Monty Bengochia, Lavina Bengochia, Amara Keller, and Jolie Varela.

Miners, including William Bodey, made camp north of Mono Lake in 1859. The camp grew into a town of more than 5,000 people by 1879, although the population declined quickly as profits fell after that. Today Bodie State Historic Park preserves 170 rustic buildings that are more than a century old.

Water wars began in the early twentieth century as Los Angeles mayor Frederick Eaton and the city's water superintendent, William Mulholland, led an effort that forever changed the Eastern Sierra. City agents bought large amounts of Owens Valley land between 1905 and 1907 before locals realized their purpose, building a 233-mile aqueduct to Southern California by 1913. Los Angeles's endless thirst drained Owens River, Owens Lake, and the farms and fields that once supported abundant crops and cattle. Incensed residents dynamited the aqueduct at least eight times, starting in 1924. In response, Los Angeles sent police armed with machine guns to guard it. The city bought more land and owned 90 percent of Owens Valley water by 1928, ending most agriculture in the region.

Under President Teddy Roosevelt, the federal government in 1907 established Inyo National Forest, which takes its name from the Paiute word meaning "dwelling place of the great spirit." The forest protects 2.1 million acres along the Eastern Sierra and includes Hoover, Ansel Adams, John Muir, Golden Trout, and South Sierra Wilderness Areas.

El Camino Sierra, the first paved road from Southern California to Bishop, opened to motorists in 1931. Today's travelers know the route as Highway 395, the main corridor through the Eastern Sierra.

By order of President Franklin Roosevelt during World War II, Manzanar War Relocation Center and nine other prison camps operated from 1942 to 1945. The Manzanar camp near Independence incarcerated 11,070 Japanese Americans who were mostly US citizens. Among them were Aiko Herzig-Yoshinaga and William Hohri. After the war, both investigated and challenged the government's authority to incarcerate Japanese Americans, pushing Congress to finally apologize and pay reparations in 1988. Today Manzanar National Historic Site keeps the memory of this injustice alive.

About 90 miles up the road, a twenty-six-year-old ski enthusiast named Dave McCoy set up the first rope tow on Mammoth Mountain in 1942. He obtained a Forest Service permit to develop the mountain as a ski area eleven years later, built a small lodge, and then added a used chairlift. Mammoth Mountain Ski Area was born, which led to the growth of Mammoth Lakes, a popular resort town. McCoy managed the ski area for more than sixty years, and turned 100 in 2015.

Meanwhile, Los Angeles extended its aqueduct and began to divert streams headed for Mono Lake in 1941. The lake lost half its water and doubled in salinity over the next fifty years. David Gaines and Sally Gaines formed Mono Lake Committee in 1978.

An Eastern Sierra sunset colors the sky.

They and other conservationists fought a ten-year legal battle to save the lake, which succeeded in 1994 when the state ordered Los Angeles to allow it to refill. Since then it's risen about half the distance to the court-ordered goal. Drained Owens Lake is still a lake in name only, but Los Angeles has made progress in containing its dust, which fouled Owens Valley air for many years.

Other significant people include Marie Louise Parcher, who in 1928 helped to create the Eastern California Museum in Independence, served as its first president, and devoted fifteen years to its development. Also from Independence, mountaineer Norman Clyde achieved more than 130 first ascents, published 1,467 articles, and assisted in multiple searches and rescues. Galen Rowell, adventurer and outdoor photographer extraordinaire, lived in nearby Bishop.

Andrea Mead Lawrence, a three-time Olympian who won two skiing golds in the 1952 Winter Games, served sixteen years as a Mono County supervisor and founded a nonprofit to promote conservation. "If you have the true Olympic spirit, you have to put it back into the world in meaningful ways," she said. Lawrence lived for forty years in the Mammoth Lakes area, which attracts world-class distance runners for high-elevation training. Among them are Deena Kastor, who won an Olympic marathon bronze medal in 2004, four-time Olympian Meb Keflezighi, who won a marathon silver medal in 2004, and Ryan Hall, who set an American men's marathon record. Also from Mammoth Lakes, rock climber John Bachar pioneered ropeless, "free solo" ascents, and snowboarder Kelly Clark competed in five Winter Olympics, winning three medals, including a gold.

Much has changed here since Mary Austin's time. But for those visiting the dramatic and fascinating Eastern Sierra, where a mountain now carries her name, her sound advice still applies: "for seeing and understanding, the best time is when you have the longest leave to stay."

VISITOR INFORMATION

Tioga Pass Road through Yosemite and other mountain passes south of Lake Tahoe are generally open from June through November, and closed to motorists in winter and spring.

Inyo National Forest has visitor centers north of Lee Vining, in Mammoth Lakes, in Bishop, and south of Lone Pine.

41. REVERSED PEAK

A pleasant and easy hike provides a scenic outing in the heart of the June Lake area and a good warm-up for more-challenging Eastern Sierra climbs.

Distance: 6 miles on a loop (all on trails)
Time: 3 to 4 hours
Difficulty: Class 2; easy to moderate
Parking: Beside Northshore Drive near June Lake

Trailhead elevation: 7,677 feet
Summit elevation: 9,459 feet
Elevation gain: 1,782 feet
Best season: June–Oct
Permits: None required

FINDING THE TRAILHEAD

From June Lake Junction on Highway 395 (10 miles south of Lee Vining), drive southwest on Highway 158 for about 3.75 miles, to Northshore Drive. Turn right, drive another 0.4 mile to a dirt pullout on the west side of the road, and park. GPS: N37 46.532' / W119 05.639'

CLIMBING THE MOUNTAIN

Hike on the dirt road that leads to a single-track trail. Here, the climbing begins, as the path curves around a ridge in a clockwise semicircle.

Continue northeast past a pond and scattered pines and aspens. The sagebrush that surrounds you will leave no doubt that you're hiking in the Eastern Sierra. You'll reach a signed trail junction after about 2 miles; turn left and ascend a second ridge to the north. Terrain flattens briefly, and then a final climb takes you to granite boulders that cap the summit. To top the highest one takes a few minutes of Class 2 scrambling.

Your summit view features a 360-degree view of the June Lake area, including Carson Peak to the south, Kuna Peak and Mount Lewis to the west, Grant Lake and Mono Lake to the north, and many other features of Inyo National Forest and Ansel Adams Wilderness.

When you descend, return to the signed trail junction and turn left to complete Reversed Trail Loop. This variation descends more directly toward Northshore Drive and then leads beside it until you reach your starting point again.

> ### SIERRA SECRETS
>
> Geologists believe that Reversed Peak split the Rush Creek Glacier that formed June Lake's horseshoe-shaped valley.

HISTORY

USGS surveyors exploring this area reported that "the ancient drainage has been reversed by the deposition of morainal debris; we have therefore called the stream draining June and Gull lakes Reversed Creek." Surveyors also named the peak after the creek, and the titles appeared on maps by 1901.

Reversed Peak

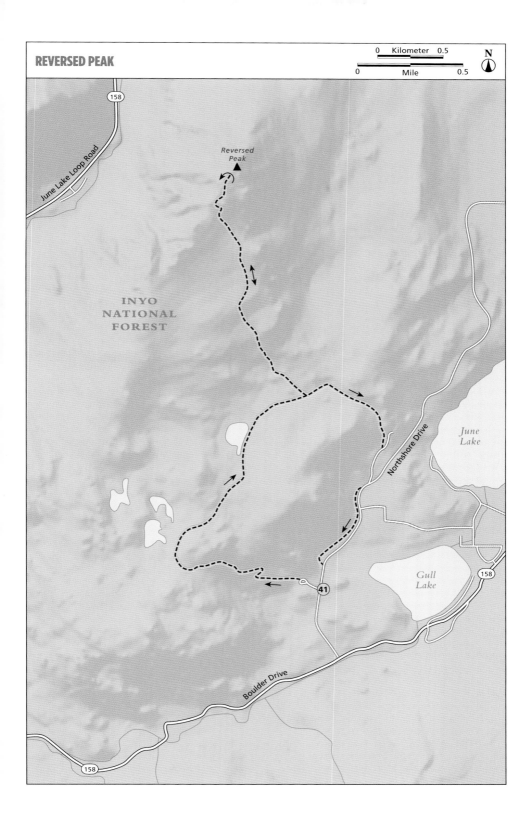

0   Kilometer   0.5

0   Mile   0.5

N

158

June Lake Loop Road

Reversed
Peak

INYO
NATIONAL
FOREST

Northshore Drive

June
Lake

Gull
Lake

158

41

Boulder Drive

158

Reversed Peak's summit looks over Ansel Adams Wilderness.

MILES AND DIRECTIONS

0.0 Hike west on a dirt road that soon becomes a trail, climbing and curving northeast

1.9 Turn left (north) at trail junction

3.2 Summit

4.5 After descending the summit spur trail to the trail junction, turn left (east)

5.0 Turn right (south) where trail meets dirt road

5.2 Take southbound trail beside Northshore Drive

6.0 Arrive back at the trailhead

42. MAMMOTH MOUNTAIN

Mammoth Mountain attracts thousands of skiers in winter and mountain bikers in summer, but what the popular peak lacks in solitude, it makes up in novelty. After an enjoyable trek through the woods near the mountain's base and up its western ridge, hikers can visit a summit station with interesting exhibits, eat at its cafe, and descend on the ski area's gondola for free.

Distance: 4 miles, one-way, with gondola descent, or 8 miles round-trip (all on trails)
Time: 3 to 4 hours with gondola descent, or 5 to 6 hours round-trip
Difficulty: Class 1; moderate (for distance and elevation gain)

Parking: Beside Highway 203/Minaret Road
Trailhead elevation: 8,921 feet
Summit elevation: 11,053 feet
Elevation gain: 2,132 feet
Best season: June–Oct
Permits: None needed

FINDING THE TRAILHEAD

Park near Mammoth Lakes Ski Area, or, to avoid traffic and parking issues, take a free bus from town. Mammoth Mountain Trail (also known as St. Anton Trail) begins on the south side of Highway 203, just west of Mammoth's Adventure Center and gondola station. GPS: N37 39.017' / W119 02.360'

CLIMBING THE MOUNTAIN

Look for short brown signposts reading "Mammoth Mountain Hiking Trail" at trail junctions throughout the ascent, and follow them carefully to avoid cycling trails and mountain bikers.

Our path begins in a forest of lodgepole pines, whitebark pines, and mountain hemlocks. In fact, a set of interpretive signs at the beginning of the trail helps hikers to identify them. The route circles around the mountain's base in a counterclockwise direction as it gains elevation. After passing above Reds Lake, the trail climbs onto Mammoth's western ridge and above the tree line. Just before the summit, we reach Lakes Basin

SIERRA SECRETS

Plenty of mountain bikers use the gondola to ride down this mountain in summer, though cyclists are not allowed to ride uphill to the summit. Mammoth requires all cyclists to buy trail passes even if they do not use the gondola.

An alternative trail leads from Twin Lakes to the summit on the Twin Lakes Trail along the mountain's western Dragons Back ridge. At around 3 miles each way, this path is slightly shorter than Mammoth Mountain Trail, but climbs around 250 feet more, and does not have the option of a gondola descent to your starting point.

An excellent spot for pictures of Mammoth Mountain as well as the Minarets is found at Minaret Vista, a few miles west of the ski area.

Mammoth Mountain

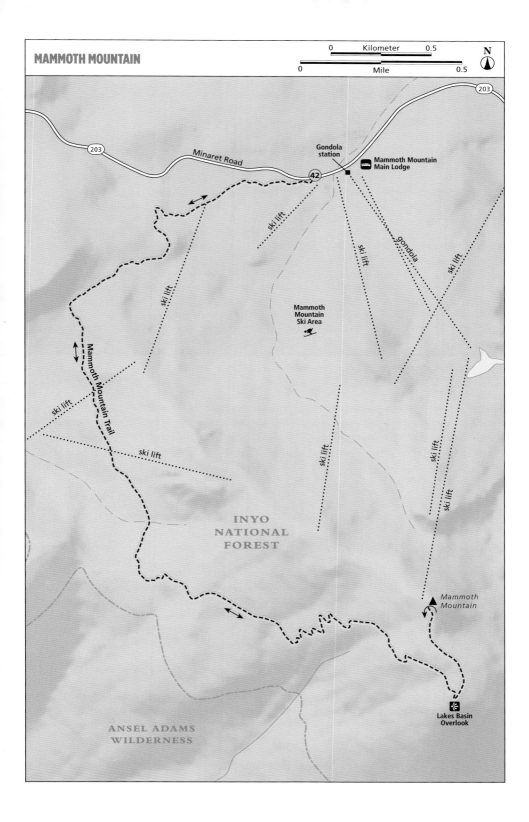

MAMMOTH MOUNTAIN

0   Kilometer   0.5

0   Mile   0.5

N

203

Minaret Road

42

Gondola station

Mammoth Mountain Main Lodge

ski lift

ski lift

gondola

ski lift

Mammoth Mountain Ski Area

ski lift

Mammoth Mountain Trail

ski lift

ski lift

ski lift

ski lift

INYO NATIONAL FOREST

Mammoth Mountain

Lakes Basin Overlook

ANSEL ADAMS WILDERNESS

Mammoth Mountain boasts an inspiring view of the Minarets, Mount Ritter, and Banner Peak.

Overlook, which deserves a stop to enjoy the southeastern view of Inyo National Forest's many lakes and peaks.

Then it's just a few hundred yards to the signed summit and Eleven53 Interpretive Center. This summit station not only commands an outstanding view of the Minarets, Mount Ritter, Banner Peak, and Devils Postpile National Monument, but also offers a variety of exhibits on local geology, wildlife, and culture. There's even a small restaurant. If you've climbed multiple mountains from this guide in a traditionally independent fashion, then you deserve to indulge in a hot lunch and a cold beer on this summit before returning effortlessly on the free gondola descent. The center and gondola close at 4:30 p.m. daily in summer and fall, or sometimes earlier, in the event of dangerous weather, such as lightning.

HISTORY

Eruptions formed this lava dome complex some 57,000 years ago. Mono Indians occupied the area exclusively until four miners staked a claim on Mineral Hill in 1877. Mammoth Mining Company formed the next year, and nearby Mammoth Mountain, Mammoth Lakes, and the future town all derive their names from that early and short-lived business. Mammoth Mountain Ski Area opened in 1953.

MILES AND DIRECTIONS

0.0 Start hiking Mammoth Mountain Trail on the south side of Highway 203 just west of Mammoth's Adventure Center. Follow short brown signs through multiple junctions as you ascend in a counterclockwise direction.

4.0 Summit

8.0 Arrive back at the trailhead

43. TRAIL PEAK

A short outing leads to a high peak with an impressive Southern Sierra view. Just a short drive from the popular Mount Whitney area, Trail Peak attracts far fewer people and requires no permits, providing a refreshing change of pace and an ideal warm-up for those planning to climb the higher mountains to the north.

Distance: 6.4 miles round-trip (on trails and cross-country)
Time: 3 to 4 hours
Difficulty: Class 2; easy to moderate (for elevation and elevation gain)
Parking: Horseshoe Meadow trailhead lot

Trailhead elevation: 9,950 feet
Summit elevation: 11,617 feet
Elevation gain: 1,667 feet
Best season: June–Oct
Permits: None needed

FINDING THE TRAILHEAD

From Highway 395 in the town of Lone Pine, turn west onto Whitney Portal Road. After 3 miles, turn left onto Horseshoe Meadows Road. Drive about 20 steep, curvy, and adventurous miles to the road's end at Horseshoe Meadow trailhead. GPS: N36 25.647' / W118 11.419'

CLIMBING THE MOUNTAIN

This is an active bear area, so use the lockers to store food from your car before departing.

Take the westbound trail toward Cottonwood Pass and Trail Pass through the woods for 0.25 mile. When you reach a junction, turn left and south, as our path emerges from the forest and crosses Horseshoe Meadow. Then the trail climbs gradually toward Trail Pass. Upon reaching it, turn right onto the Pacific Crest Trail. We are now traversing the north slope of the mountain. After about 0.5 mile, start climbing toward its summit on your left. There is no use trail to the peak, so you will have to choose your own cross-country route. Enjoy the rare foxtail pines that can live more than 2,000 years. As you climb above the tree line, there will be a few boulders to navigate, light scrambling, and a few false summits near the top.

Our summit is one of the highest points of the surrounding Kern Plateau. From here, we can view the Great Western Divide to the west and Cirque Peak and Mount Langley to the northwest. Horseshoe Meadow stretches out beneath us to the north; from this perspective you can see the aptness of its name.

HISTORY

Members of the US Geological Survey apparently named the mountain in 1905. John Hockett (1828–1898) from Arkansas pioneered the Hockett Trail that crosses the range and climbs over Trail Pass in the 1860s; his name also applies to meadows, lakes, a creek, and a mountain in the Southern Sierra. Congress designated this area as Golden Trout Wilderness in 1978 to protect the small and beautiful fish that inhabit its high streams and lakes.

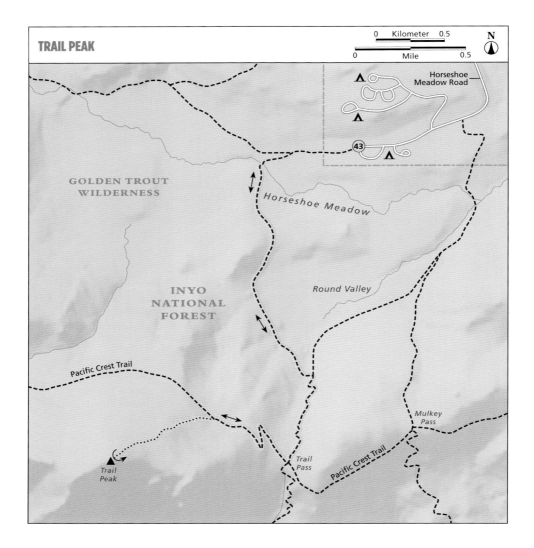

0   Kilometer   0.5
0   Mile   0.5

N

Horseshoe
Meadow Road

43

GOLDEN TROUT
WILDERNESS

Horseshoe Meadow

INYO
NATIONAL
FOREST

Round Valley

Pacific Crest Trail

Mulkey
Pass

Trail
Peak

Trail
Pass

Pacific Crest Trail

SIERRA SECRETS

Golden trout are native to the Southern Sierra, including the South Fork of the Kern River and Golden Trout Creek. Overfishing, interbreeding, and cattle grazing in their habitat made the Little Kern golden trout a threatened subspecies in 1978. The wilderness refuge reduces threats to their habitat, and the government has removed at least some of the hybrid fish that jeopardized their breeding. Anglers should be sure to observe fishing limits and restrictions.

The trailhead is more than 6,200 feet higher than the nearby town of Lone Pine, and the summit stands 1,667 feet higher still. Beware of headaches that come with rapid elevation gain, especially if you've just arrived from sea level.

Trail Peak's summit reveals Horseshoe Meadow and Golden Trout Wilderness.

MILES AND DIRECTIONS

0.0 Start at Horseshoe Meadow trailhead and hike west

0.2 At trail junction, turn left (south)

2.2 At Trail Pass, turn right (west) onto the Pacific Crest Trail

2.7 Leave PCT, climbing cross-country to the left (southwest), toward the summit

3.2 Summit

6.4 Arrive back at the trailhead

44. MOUNT STARR

Discover the marvelously scenic Rock Creek area on this hike in the heart of John Muir Wilderness. A half-day ascent leads beside and above pristine lakes and atop an impressive mountain surrounded by other picturesque summits.

Distance: 7.8 miles round-trip (all on trails)
Time: 3 to 5 hours
Difficulty: Class 2; moderate to strenuous (for distance, elevation, and elevation gain)

Parking: Mosquito Flat trailhead
Trailhead elevation: 10,130 feet
Summit elevation: 12,835 feet
Elevation gain: 2,705 feet
Best season: June–Oct
Permits: None needed

FINDING THE TRAILHEAD

From Toms Place on Highway 395, drive southwest on Rock Creek Road for 11 miles until the road ends at Mosquito Flat trailhead in Little Lakes Valley. GPS: N37 26.114' / W118 44.827'

CLIMBING THE MOUNTAIN

Mount Starr and its long summit ridge stand right above the parking area to the southwest. Our trail leads south and right along its base as we start to gain elevation right away. Mack Lake is the first point of interest. Here we find a trail junction; take the right fork toward Mono Pass. As you climb, you may be tempted to ascend the mountain's eastern slope on use trails, or cross-country. This does make for a shorter but steeper ascent that's more taxing and less pleasant than the western slope.

Soon we climb above the tree line and ascend sandy switchbacks. The next trail junction arrives at pretty Ruby Lake, which is worth a 0.25-mile detour to the left; but for a direct ascent, stay right for Mono Pass. Terrain steepens here and snow may fill this gully even in summer, especially after a big winter.

Once over the pass, you'll see Mount Starr's western slope on your right. Look for a use trail leading to the summit ridge, or if snow still covers the peak, pick your own line. The long summit ridge has multiple high points; the true summit stands near the middle.

Our view of Inyo National Forest includes Wheeler Ridge and Little Lakes Valley to the east, and four "13ers" to the south: Mount Mills, Mount Abbot, Mount Dade, and Mount Morgan.

To descend, you could simply reverse your steps as usual. This would make for

SIERRA SECRETS

At more than 10,000 feet, this is the highest starting point of any climb in this guide. For that reason, it's a good idea to spend some time in the Eastern Sierra and climb a lower mountain or two before attempting this one.

On the way in or out, you may want to stop to enjoy Rock Creek Lake, which has a campground. There are ten other campgrounds along Rock Creek Road between Toms Place and Mosquito Flat trailhead.

a 7.8-mile outing. Another option is to go down the eastern slope and rejoin the trail above Mack Lake, making a loop trip. This terrain is steeper and might not be suitable for beginners or children. But for those comfortable going off-trail, it does add variety, and cuts about 2 miles off the return trip.

Most Eastern Sierra visitors speed up and down Highway 395 between Mammoth Lakes and Bishop without ever turning onto side roads like this one. If you're one of them, come take a look; one visit will make you wish you'd come sooner.

HISTORY

Walter Starr Sr. and Allen Chickering made the first recorded ascent on July 16, 1896, when a thunderstorm alarmed the pair. "Suddenly everything began to buzz . . . The camera tripod, our fingertips, and even our hair, which stood out straight, seemed to exude electricity. We were badly frightened, and got off the peak as rapidly as possible," they wrote. They named the mountain Electric Peak. But the Sierra Club later renamed the summit in honor of Walter Starr Jr. (1903–1933), a mountaineer, guidebook author, and lawyer who died while climbing in the Minarets.

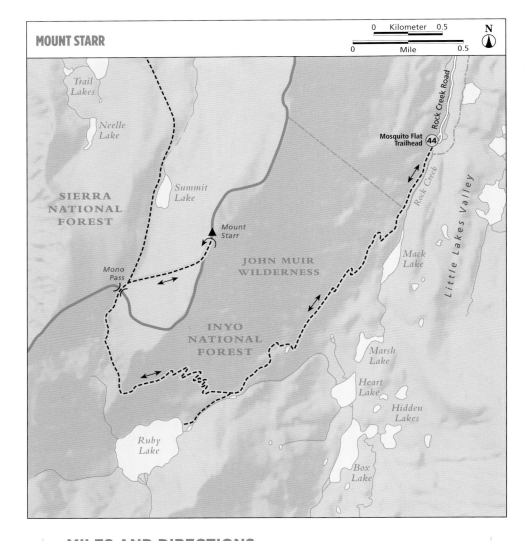

MILES AND DIRECTIONS

0.0 Start at Mosquito Flat trailhead and hike southwest

0.5 Stay right (southwest) at Mack Lake and Morgan Pass/Mono Pass trail junction

1.9 Turn right (west) at Ruby Lake/Mono Pass trail junction and climb up switchbacks as the path turns north

3.2 At Mono Pass, leave the main trail and take a use trail to the right (northeast), toward the summit

3.9 Summit

7.8 Arrive back at the trailhead

45. MOUNT DANA

Mount Dana provides an excellent opportunity for high-altitude climbing without the time, toil, and gear that most big mountains require. Thanks to a high trailhead at Tioga Pass, this is probably the most easily reached of California's 147 peaks that are at least 13,000 feet tall. The use trail to the summit is fairly easy to follow when not covered by snow.

Distance: 5.6 miles round-trip (on trails and use trails)
Time: 4 to 6 hours
Difficulty: Class 2; strenuous (for elevation and elevation gain)
Parking: Beside Highway 120 near Tioga Pass

Trailhead elevation: 9,943 feet
Summit elevation: 13,057 feet
Elevation gain: 3,114 feet
Best season: June–Oct
Permits: None needed

FINDING THE TRAILHEAD

Park beside Highway 120 just outside Yosemite's Tioga Pass entrance station, about 13 miles from Lee Vining. If approaching from the east, it's not necessary to drive into the park (and pay the entrance fee). GPS: N37 54.652' / W119 15.467'

CLIMBING THE MOUNTAIN

Find the path leading east from the kiosk and across Dana Meadows. Trees quickly give way to grass, which soon gives way to an endless sea of metamorphic rock. Now the climb steepens, and switchbacks begin up the mountain's western slope.

Our climb eases briefly at a plateau at about 11,500 feet. Once here, you've gained half the elevation between the trailhead and summit. Several use paths lead upward; try to follow the one along the ridgeline. The last part of the climb is the steepest, and you will have to scramble over rocks on the final approach.

SIERRA SECRETS

Don't let the short distance fool you: Mount Dana is a tall peak that requires climbers to acclimate before ascending. Drink plenty of water and have aspirin or ibuprofen handy.

Also named for James Dana are a ridge on the moon, a crater on Mars, and the rare mineral danalite.

Snow makes route finding more difficult, but also allows glissading in the right conditions. Before attempting to slide down snow, make sure you're on a gentle slope with soft snow, and equipped with an ice ax. Don't try to glissade down steep or icy slopes, especially above rocks.

Mount Dana

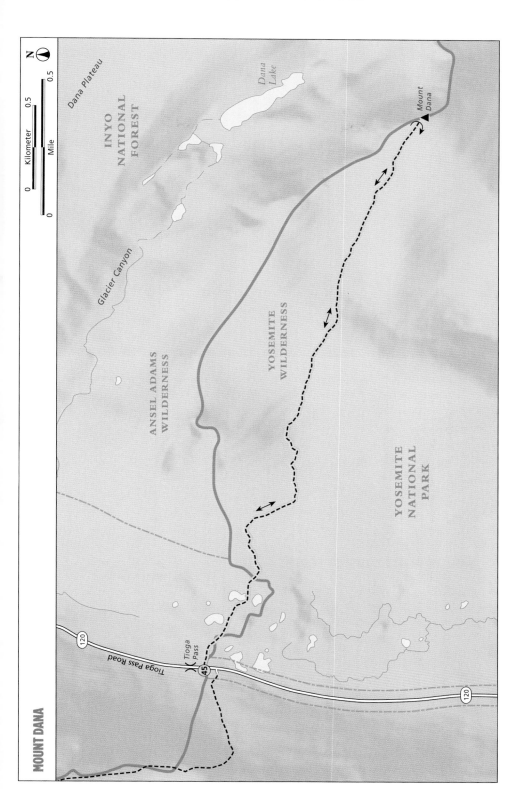

MOUNT DANA

Dana Plateau

INYO
NATIONAL
FOREST

Dana
Lake

Glacier Canyon

Mount
Dana

YOSEMITE
WILDERNESS

ANSEL ADAMS
WILDERNESS

YOSEMITE
NATIONAL
PARK

120

Tioga Pass Road

Tioga
Pass

45

120

N

0   Kilometer   0.5

0   Mile   0.5

Our summit view includes Mono Lake to the east and a vast array of Sierra Nevada mountains as far as the eye can see to the north and south. You'd have to work hard to find a better vista than this one, so stay a while.

HISTORY

William Brewer and Charles Hoffmann of the Whitney Survey made the first recorded ascent on June 28, 1863. The two named the mountain after prominent geologist James Dana (1813–1895). Brewer was so impressed with the vista that he climbed the peak again the next day, this time with Josiah Whitney, who called the view the "grandest ever beheld."

MILES AND DIRECTIONS

0.0   Start from Tioga Pass entrance station and hike east across Dana Meadows

0.5   Continue west as the route becomes a use trail, ascending Mount Dana's western slope

2.8   Summit

5.6   Arrive back at the trailhead

46. MOUNT CONNESS

Mount Conness, visible from much of Yosemite's high country, beckons many hikers and climbers. This mountain straddling Yosemite and Inyo National Forest requires stamina, route-finding skills, and an ascent of Class 3 terrain with intimidating exposure near the summit. Those who overcome these challenges reach the highest Sierra Nevada summit north of Highway 120.

Distance: 8 miles round-trip (on trails and cross-country)
Time: 6 to 8 hours
Difficulty: Class 3; strenuous (for length, terrain, elevation, and elevation gain)

Parking: Beside Saddlebag Lake Road near Sawmill Campground
Trailhead elevation: 9,842 feet
Summit elevation: 12,590 feet
Elevation gain: 2,748 feet
Best season: July–Sept
Permits: None needed

FINDING THE TRAILHEAD

Find Saddlebag Lake Road from Highway 120, about 2 miles east of Tioga Pass. Turn north onto it and drive 1.6 miles to Sawmill Campground. Park beside the road (the camp lot is only for registered campers). GPS: N37 57.347' / W119 15.979'

CLIMBING THE MOUNTAIN

Our route leads through the camp and then beside Lee Vining Creek. Follow the trail west beneath the mountain's eastern flank. Pass through a wooded valley with a stream and wildflowers in the grassy meadow near the Carnegie Institute research hut.

As you begin to ascend to steeper terrain, the route becomes less clear. Climb above the tree line on a use trail that leads up the mountain's rocky southeast ridge; be aware that snow may conceal the path in early season. Climb to the west, to the eastern shore of Alpine Lake, passing it above the north shore. After you gain the ridge above you, Conness Lakes and Conness Glacier come into view to the north.

Once you reach the summit plateau, look west to see the summit at the top of a narrow and rocky ridge, which is the crux of the route. This final obstacle contains Class 2 and 3 terrain, with steep drops on either side, commanding your full attention. Exposure like this isn't for everyone, and has turned plenty of climbers back, so stay within your limits and make a good decision.

Our rewarding summit view features Mount Dana, Mount Lyell, and Mount Maclure to the south, Tuolumne Meadows to the west, Sawtooth Ridge to the north, and Saddlebag Lake to the east.

HISTORY

Members of the Whitney Survey named the mountain for John Conness (1821–1909), who helped approve the survey in the Legislature, served in the US Senate, and also helped establish Yosemite Valley as a national park. Clarence King and James Gardiner made the first known ascent in 1864.

Mount Conness

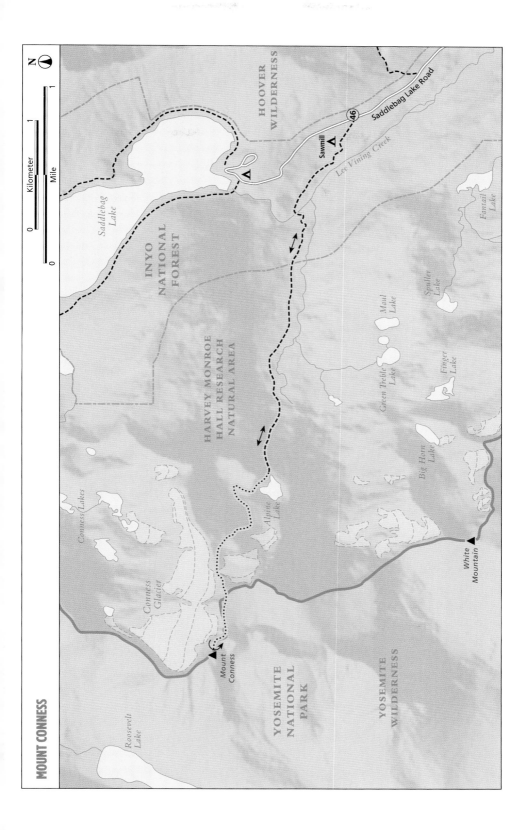

MOUNT CONNESS

N

Kilometer
0   1

Mile
0   1

Saddlebag
Lake

Saddlebag Lake Road

46

Sawmill

Lee Vining Creek

HOOVER
WILDERNESS

INYO
NATIONAL
FOREST

HARVEY MONROE
HALL RESEARCH
NATURAL AREA

Fantail
Lake

Spuller
Lake

Maul
Lake

Green Treble
Lake

Finger
Lake

Big Horn
Lake

Conness Lakes

Conness Glacier

Roosevelt
Lake

Alpine
Lake

Mount
Conness

White
Mountain

YOSEMITE
NATIONAL
PARK

YOSEMITE
WILDERNESS

A full moon drops behind the summit of Mount Conness.

MILES AND DIRECTIONS

0.0   Start at Sawmill Campground and hike west

1.0   Pass Carnegie Institute research hut and continue west

2.0   Pass north of Alpine Lake and continue west

4.0   Summit

8.0   Arrive back at the trailhead

SIERRA SECRETS

John Conness, an Irish-born immigrant, compiled a record of public service that has aged well. As a US senator, he voted for the Thirteenth, Fourteenth, and Fifteenth Amendments, which abolished slavery and granted citizenship and suffrage to former slaves. His support of Chinese immigration and civil rights placed him ahead of his time, although those positions cost him public support, and his office.

Climbers need altitude acclimation to ascend tall peaks like Mount Conness. Spend a few days in a high area like Tuolumne Meadows before taking it on.

Plan for snow: Mount Conness normally keeps its winter coat well into mid-season.

47. HURD PEAK

An impressive summit with a short approach makes this an appealing adventure. Launching from a trailhead nearly 10,000 feet high makes it possible to climb a High Sierra peak and return in about half a day, though the ascent is a physical one.

Distance: 6 miles round-trip (on trails and cross-country)
Time: 4 to 6 hours
Difficulty: Class 2 or 3; strenuous (for distance, elevation, and elevation gain)

Parking: South Lake lot
Trailhead elevation: 9,829 feet
Summit elevation: 12,237 feet
Elevation gain: 2,408 feet
Best season: June–Oct
Permits: None needed

FINDING THE TRAILHEAD

From Bishop, drive southwest on Highway 168 for about 15 miles. Then turn left onto South Lake Road and drive another 6 miles to South Lake. Park in the day-use area. GPS: N37 10.138' / W118 33.966'

CLIMBING THE MOUNTAIN

There are countless ways to ascend this mountain. The big question climbers must answer first is whether to approach the east or west face. The east face has a 2-mile approach to Long Lake and a Class 2–3 ascent. The west face has a 2.5-mile approach to Treasure Lakes and a climb that's consistently Class 3. Most opt for the shorter hike and easier ascent. Either way, expect lots of sand, gravel, and rock hopping.

For the east face, take the southbound Bishop Pass Trail. Stay left and head for Bishop Pass at the trail junction in about 0.75 mile. You will see the mountain from the parking lot and on most of the approach. Once at Long Lake, it will stand on your right. There is no marked trail to the summit, though many climb the most visible chute. Leave the Bishop Pass Trail at the lake's northernmost point, traverse the lake's west bank, and pick your own line upward.

For the west face, still take the Bishop Pass Trail, but turn right toward Treasure Lakes at the junction. The route meanders westward before turning south and climbing to the lakes. As on the east face, there is no marked summit route, so traverse the lakes and choose your own path up. This side of the mountain has large granite sub-peaks on the northwest flank that can look like the real summit from below them. Climbers can avoid these (and their Class 4 or even Class 5 terrain) by traversing above the easternmost lake before ascending a steep gully.

> **SIERRA SECRETS**
>
> Whichever way you ascend the mountain, you can descend on the opposite side and make your outing into a loop.
>
> If you ascend or descend the east face, a sweet hike around Chocolate Peak only adds about 2 miles to your outing.

Hurd Peak

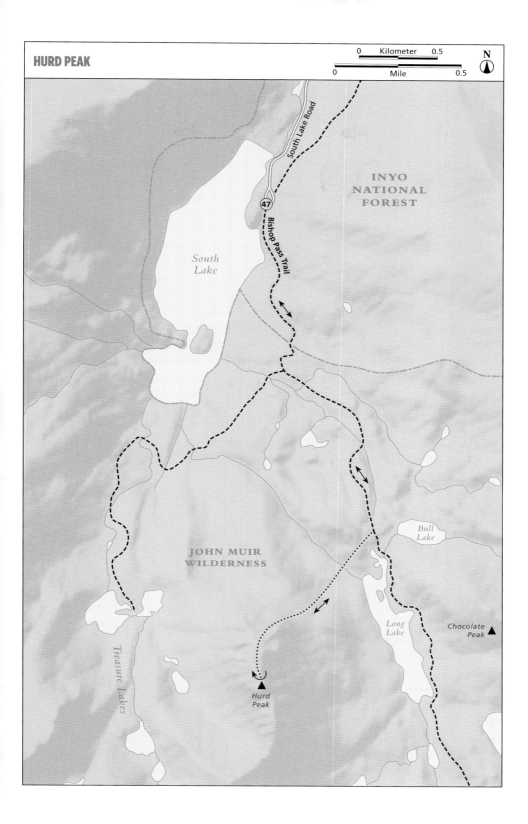

0   Kilometer   0.5

0   Mile   0.5

N

South Lake Road

INYO
NATIONAL
FOREST

47

Bishop Pass Trail

*South
Lake*

*Bull
Lake*

JOHN MUIR
WILDERNESS

Treasure Lakes

*Long
Lake*

Chocolate ▲
Peak

▲
*Hurd
Peak*

There are several high points on the summit ridge; the true summit is on the south end of it. Our view includes dozens of peaks and lakes from John Muir Wilderness, Inyo National Forest, and Kings Canyon National Park, including the dramatic Inconsolable Range to the east.

Both east and west faces hold plenty of loose rock, so watch your step on the descent and keep some distance between parties.

HISTORY

H. C. Hurd, a US government engineer, made the first known ascent in 1906, "while making certain explorations of this region." William Colby suggested naming the mountain for Hurd in 1920, and the name appeared on maps by 1923. A small lake north of the peak also bears his name.

MILES AND DIRECTIONS

0.0   For the east face ascent, start at South Lake trailhead and hike south on Bishop Pass Trail

0.75   Turn left (east) at junction to stay on Bishop Pass Trail

2.0   At the north end of Long Lake, turn right (southwest) to leave the trail and ascend the east face of the mountain

3.0   Summit

6.0   Arrive back at the trailhead

48. **LONE PINE PEAK**

The mountain that looks so big and impressive from the town of Lone Pine is not Mount Whitney, as many wrongly assume, but Lone Pine Peak. Compared to its popular neighbor, this summit offers a shorter hike, fewer hikers, and no permit requirements for day use.

Distance: 10.4 miles (on trails and cross-country)
Time: 6 to 8 hours
Difficulty: Class 2; strenuous (for distance, elevation, and elevation gain)

Parking: Meysan Lake trailhead lot
Trailhead elevation: 8,049 feet
Summit elevation: 12,949 feet
Elevation gain: 4,900 feet
Best season: June–Oct
Permits: None needed

FINDING THE TRAILHEAD

 From Lone Pine, drive toward Whitney Portal near the end of Whitney Portal Road. Look for a Meysan Lake trailhead parking sign just east of Whitney Portal Campground and park here. GPS: N36 35.275' / W118 13.501'

CLIMBING THE MOUNTAIN

Be careful not to follow most hikers heading for Mount Whitney from its trailhead at the road's end. From the Meysan Lake trailhead parking area, walk south and east through the campground and follow the signs for about 0.5 mile to Meysan Lake Trail; there will be a number of turns leading through the camp and past private cabins.

Our trail climbs steeply through the canyon above Meysan Creek, which will likely roar throughout your ascent. Enjoy the variety of trees as you gain elevation, passing jeffrey pines, pinion pines, and finally, the rare and beautiful foxtail pines, which are native to the southeast Sierra and can live more than 2,000 years. Admiring them provides a welcome diversion from the switchbacks.

After about 4 miles, our path levels off and we reach Grass Lake. The trail continues toward Meysan Lake, but our route leaves it here and continues cross-country. Hike south beside Grass Lake and turn to the southeast, aiming for a chute beneath the saddle between Lone Pine Peak and Peak 3985. Next comes the crux as we ascend the northwest-facing slope using that chute of talus and scree. This climb will test your strength, but also keeps the crowds away. Once you reach the saddle, the summit lies 0.6 mile to the northeast.

Looking over and far beyond John Muir Wilderness and Inyo National Forest, you will see one of the best views in the entire mountain range, including five of California's "14ers," including (from north to south) Mount Williamson, Mount Russell, Mount Whitney, Mount Muir, and Mount Langley.

HISTORY

Paiute originally called the mountain *Opopago*. But a single pine tree growing near the Eastern Sierra community established in the 1860s inspired the name of the town, its nearby creek, and the mountain that towers above them both. A storm toppled the lone

Lone Pine Peak

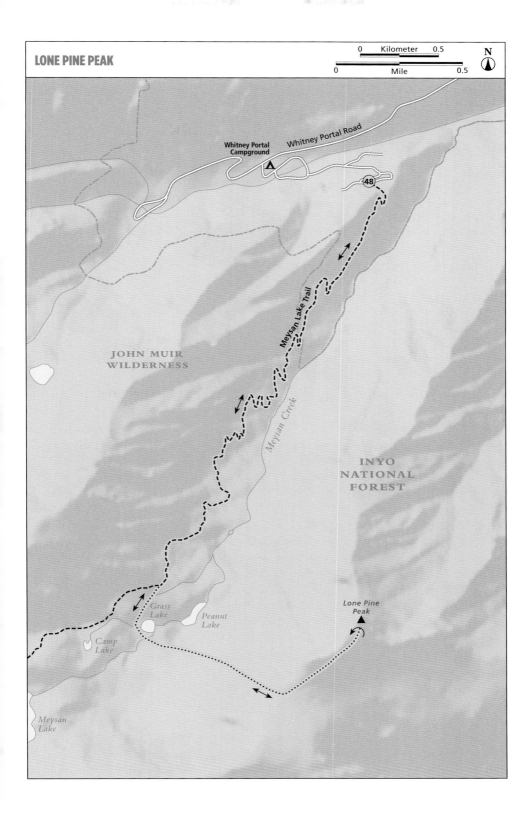

pine in 1876. Mountaineer Norman Clyde (1885–1972) made the first known ascent in 1925.

SIERRA SECRETS

The recommended chute can be easy to miss on the descent; from the summits, it's the third one you will see to the southwest.

Snow in late spring and early summer can make the ascent up the northwest slope's scree and talus much easier, and more enjoyable.

If you decide to make an overnight trip, Grass Lake, Camp Lake, and Meysan Lake provide excellent camping sites.

MILES AND DIRECTIONS

0.0 Park beside Whitney Portal Road at the signed Meysan Lake trailhead lot and walk south and east through the campground, following signs for Meysan Lake Trail

0.5 At the Meysan Lake trailhead, hike south as the trail starts climbing

4.0 Leave the trail at Grass Lake, hiking cross-country or on a use trail to the southeast, then climb steeply to a saddle beside Lone Pine Peak

4.6 At the saddle, hike northeast toward the summit

5.2 Summit

10.4 Arrive back at the trailhead

Climbers atop Lone Pine Peak can view Owens Valley and the summits looming above it.

49. **MOUNT GOULD**

A well-maintained trail through John Muir Wilderness takes hikers within striking distance of a highly scenic peak at the edge of Kings Canyon National Park. From Kearsarge Pass, climbers ascend the mountain's steep southern slope off-trail to a granite summit block. This is a good workout, but fast and doable as "13ers" go.

Distance: 10.2 miles (on trails and cross-country)	**Trailhead elevation:** 9,200 feet
	Summit elevation: 13,005 feet
Time: 6 to 8 hours	**Elevation gain:** 3,805 feet
Difficulty: Class 3; strenuous (for elevation, elevation gain, and terrain)	**Best season:** June–Oct
	Permits: None needed
Parking: Onion Valley lot	

FINDING THE TRAILHEAD

From Independence, drive west on Onion Valley Road for 13 miles to a large parking area. Kearsarge Pass trailhead is located to the west, between the bathrooms and campground. GPS: N36 46.365' / W118 20.441'

CLIMBING THE MOUNTAIN

Hike west on Kearsarge Pass Trail (labeled Bubbs Creek Trail on some maps) as it climbs up switchbacks past several picturesque lakes. The best of these for resting and getting water is Gilbert Lake; visiting the others requires detouring off the trail. Our hike leads through a forest of beautiful foxtail pines, which are found only in the Southern Sierra, and can live for thousands of years. Enjoy them before the trail climbs above the tree line.

Pause at Kearsarge Pass to enjoy gazing into Kings Canyon National Park. Then leave the trail, climbing north up Class 2 terrain on the mountain's south slope. There is no maintained trail, though you may find use trails of climbers who have gone before. If not, aim for the highest visible point, but don't be discouraged when it turns out to be a false summit. There are a few of these! You will know when you spot the true summit, which is a pointy granite formation. Walking to its base involves more Class 2 terrain; to stand atop it requires a few Class 3 moves. Either way, you will enjoy a panoramic view that includes Kearsarge Peak, Mount Mary Austin, Golden Trout Lake, University Peak, and much more.

HISTORY

Joseph LeConte and three others made the first recorded ascent on July 20, 1890. They named the mountain "University Peak" after the University of California at Berkeley, where LeConte studied. But four years later, LeConte and different companions climbed a higher peak to the south and decided to honor Cal there instead. That second mountain is now called "University Peak," and LeConte renamed his earlier conquest after Wilson Gould, a member of the second climbing party.

Mount Gould

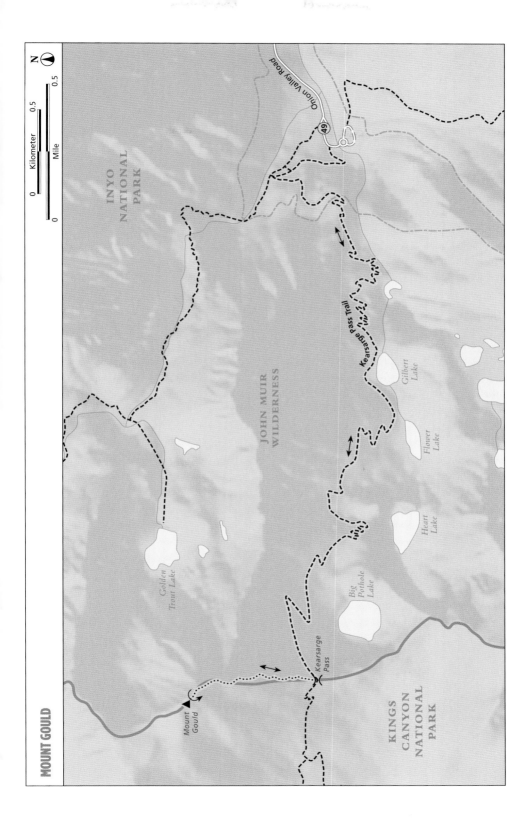

MOUNT GOULD

N

| 0 | Kilometer | 0.5 | 0.5 |

| 0 | Mile | 0.5 |

INYO
NATIONAL
PARK

Orion Valley Road

49

Kearsarge Pass Trail

Gilbert Lake

Flower Lake

JOHN MUIR
WILDERNESS

Heart Lake

Big Pothole Lake

Golden Trout Lake

Kearsarge Pass

Mount Gould

KINGS
CANYON
NATIONAL
PARK

Mount Gould's summit allows climbers to look deep into Kings Canyon National Park.

MILES AND DIRECTIONS

0.0 Park at the end of Onion Valley Road, walk west to the signed Kearsarge Pass trailhead, and start hiking west

0.4 Stay left (southwest) at trail junction

4.6 At Kearsarge Pass, turn right (north) and leave the trail to climb the mountain's south face

5.1 Summit

10.2 Arrive back at the trailhead

SIERRA SECRETS

The names of Kearsarge Pass and nearby Kearsarge Peak refer to a Civil War–era US battleship that sank the Confederate ship *Alabama* in 1864. When hearing of the *Kearsarge* victory, Union supporters applied its name to a mining town (which an avalanche destroyed in 1866), and eventually, to the pass and mountain, "to taunt the Rebels."

50. MOUNT WHITNEY

Hikers can stand atop the highest mountain in the Lower 48 and return in a single rigorous day, making this both a popular adventure and a tough permit to obtain. But there are alternatives to the single-day outing that provide other permitting options. Mount Whitney marks the southern end of the John Muir Trail, providing a thrilling start or finish for those hiking the entire 210-mile adventure.

Distance: 21 miles round-trip (all on trails)
Time: 12 to 15 hours
Difficulty: Class 2; strenuous (for distance, elevation, and elevation gain)

Parking: Whitney Portal lot
Trailhead elevation: 8,300 feet
Summit elevation: 14,505 feet
Elevation gain: 6,205 feet
Best season: July–Sept
Permits: Required

FINDING THE TRAILHEAD

From Lone Pine, take Whitney Portal Road to its end and park. Find the trailhead to the east of the store and cafe. GPS: N36 35.215' / W118 14.394'

GETTING THE PERMIT

Planning ahead is the key idea here. Tens of thousands of people want to climb Mount Whitney each year—so many that Inyo National Forest holds an annual permit lottery. Your chances of getting a date are still fairly good, but you must submit your first choice and alternate dates between February 1 and March 15 at recreation.gov. A nonrefundable application fee applies. Forest officials conduct the lottery in late March and post results online by April 1. Hikers then have until April 30 to accept their offered dates and pay a fee (per group member). To pick up the permit, group leaders will have to visit the Eastern Sierra Interagency Visitor Center, 2 miles south of Lone Pine on Highway 395, before their climb begins. Inyo issues 100 day-use and 60 overnight permits per day between May 1 and November 1. Between day-use and overnight requests, lottery applications are 35 percent successful, but that figure increases significantly when alternate dates are included.

If you miss the lottery, you can still check for openings at recreation.gov (single climbers or small groups may find something mid-week), or for last-minute cancellations at the visitor center.

CLIMBING THE MOUNTAIN

Let's start with some tips to help you make the most of your outing, because this climb is equally great and difficult; informed observers estimate first-timers' summit rate at around 50 percent. Only those in excellent physical shape will succeed in hiking 21 miles while gaining and descending more than 6,000 feet in a single day. If that's not you, then strongly consider overnight options at Outpost Camp or Trail Camp. For many, this is not just physically easier but also quite a bit more fun. Pack light, but don't go without essential items. Human waste kit bags (provided with your permit) are imperative to take

SIERRA SECRETS

Those with time but no day-use permit have several options. Shortest of these is the Mount Whitney Mountaineers' Route, which consists of hiking beside the North Fork of Lone Pine Creek to Iceberg Lake and ascending the gully on the eastern flank. This snowy or icy route requires crampons, ice axes, the ability to use them, and about three days. Though just 15 miles, this Class 3 route is not for beginners. Other starting points include Horseshoe Meadow (three to four days) or Onion Valley (four to five days). All of these variations require permits, but they should be easier to get than those for the main route.

Eastern Sierra locals who disliked Whitney later suggested naming the mountain "Fisherman's Peak," but the effort failed.

Smithsonian astronomers built the summit's stone hut over four weeks in 1909; it once housed a state-of-the-art telescope.

LeRoy Jeffers made the first recorded ascent of nearby Mount Muir on April 30, 1927.

A US Navy ship carries the mountain's name. Launched in 1970, the USS *Mount Whitney* ports in Italy.

and carry back; there are no longer toilets anywhere on the trail. All climbers should take headlamps or flashlights even if they plan to get back before dark. Odds are, they will need them to either leave or return (or both) in darkness. Backpackers need bear canisters to protect their food. Acclimating to the altitude, eating well, and hydrating adequately will likely make the difference between reaching the summit or not. Finally, build up to this one and don't make it your first big climb at high elevation.

Still want to go? Good! Follow the trail that starts at the end of the road. Steady climbing starts right away on switchbacks as the path crosses Carillon Creek and North Fork of Lone Pine Creek. Lone Pine Lake and the meadow called Bighorn Park will appear next, followed by Outpost Camp, the first of two sites supporting overnight climbers. At 10,360 feet of elevation, Outpost is warmer and more hospitable than the higher Trail Camp, located 2.5 miles away, but reaching the higher camp on your first day will make summit day shorter and easier. Switchbacks climb to pretty Mirror Lake. Then Lone Pine Creek runs beside the trail until Trail Camp and the pond beside it. This is the last reliable source of water, so have a drink and fill up.

Now the serious climbing begins on the mountain's notorious ninety-nine switchbacks that gain about 1,700 feet over the next 2 miles. This is the steepest and most difficult part of the climb, so take your time. When you reach Trail Crest, you'll enter Sequoia National Park. Soon we reach the John Muir Trail junction. To the left is Guitar Lake and the long path to Yosemite. Our route lies to the right, and the summit is less than 2 miles away.

Now the last thing most people want to do at this point is add more climbing to the day, but a rare opportunity approaches. Our trail passes within 0.25 mile and 250 vertical feet of Mount Muir's summit, 14,019 feet tall. Adding a Class 3 scramble to bag another peak may not appeal to those already pushing their limits, but experienced climbers may jump at the chance to top another California "14er" for fairly little additional effort.

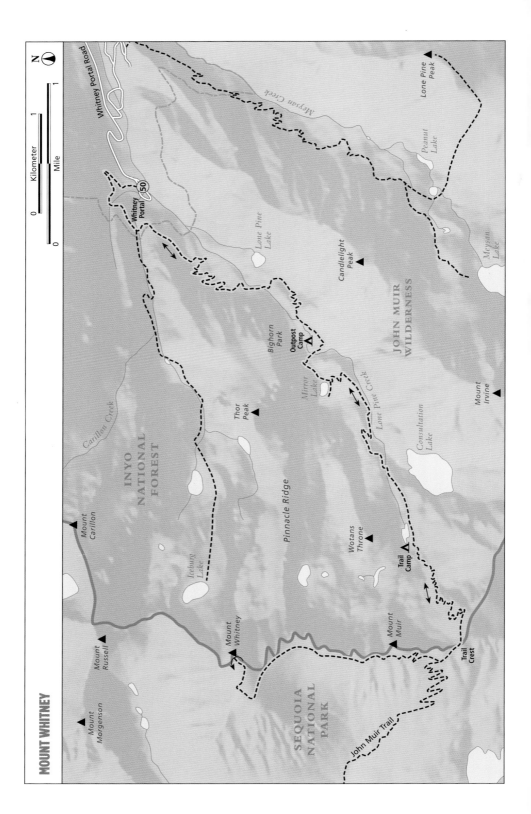